W9-BIM-766

Reframing PTSD as Traumatic Grief

ALSO BY ALAN D. WOLFELT, PH.D., C.T.

Companioning the Bereaved:
A Soulful Guide for Caregivers

Healing Your Traumatized Heart:
100 Practical Ideas After Someone You Love
Dies a Sudden, Violent Death

Living in the Shadow of the Ghosts of Grief

The Mourner's Book of Hope:
30 Days of Inspiration

Understanding Your Grief:
Ten Essential Touchstones for
Finding Hope and Healing Your Heart

Companion Press is dedicated to the education and support of both the bereaved and bereavement caregivers. We believe that those who companion the bereaved by walking with them as they journey in grief have a wondrous opportunity: to help others embrace and grow through grief— and to lead fuller, more deeply-lived lives themselves because of this important ministry.

For a complete catalog and ordering information, write, call, or visit:

Companion Press
The Center for Loss and Life Transition
3735 Broken Bow Road | Fort Collins, CO 80526
(970) 226-6050 | www.centerforloss.com

Reframing PTSD as Traumatic Grief

HOW CAREGIVERS CAN

Companion

TRAUMATIZED GRIEVERS THROUGH

CATCH-UP MOURNING

ALAN D. WOLFELT, PH.D., C.T.

Companion Press is an imprint of the Center for Loss and Life Transition,
3735 Broken Bow Road, Fort Collins, Colorado 80526.

Companion Press books may be purchased in bulk for sales promotions, premiums, and fundraisers. Please contact the publisher at the above address for more information.

21 20 19 18 17 16 15 14 5 4 3 2 1

ISBN: 978-1-61722-213-9

To all for whom the cloud of PTSD has not yet lifted.

There can be light.

My hope is that this resource will help inspire

caregivers to provide you with a safe place

in which to surrender to the

wilderness that is traumatic grief.

Contents

FOREWORD 1

INTRODUCTION 5

The soul of grief. 6

De-pathologizing PTSD 7

The missing piece? Mourning. 8

Thank you 10

CHAPTER ONE:

Grief not as an illness but as a response to injury 11

Terms used in this book 14

CHAPTER TWO:

Traumatic loss and grief. 15

What is PTSD? 18

PTSD by the numbers 19

The inciting event, or "stressor". 20

Inciting events in PTSD 21

PTSD and the military 22

PTSD sub-types. 23

CHAPTER THREE:

The symptoms of PTSD and traumatic grief. 25

PTSD symptoms 25

Uncomplicated grief symptoms 26

Shock, numbness, denial, and disbelief 26

Disorganization, confusion, searching, and yearning 27

Anxiety, panic, and fear. 27

Explosive emotions 28

Guilt and regret 28

Sadness and depression 29

Relief 29

"Comorbidities" in PTSD 29

PTSD versus grief. 31

Traumatic grief 32

Care-eliciting symptoms 34

PTSD versus operational stress injury 35

CHAPTER FOUR:
The fear factor of PTSD 37
PTSD and the brain. 38
A "disease" of memory 39
Is PTSD an inherited predisposition? 40
Can—and should—we *prevent* traumatic memories? 41
PTSD and the biological/spiritual chasm 42

CHAPTER FIVE:
Fear, withdrawal, and negativity in normal grief 45
Fear in normal grief 45
Avoidance and emotional/spiritual withdrawal in normal grief. 48
Negative cognition and mood in normal grief 50

CHAPTER SIX:
Traumatic grief as a form of complicated grief 53
Ten factors that can contribute to complicated grief. 54
1. The specific circumstances of the loss 54
2. The griever's personality, including the ability to understand and access emotionality 55
PTSD: Risk factors and resilience 56
3. In the case of the death of someone loved, the griever's relationship with the person who died 57
4. The griever's access to and use of support systems. 57
5. The griever's cultural/ethnic background 57
6. The griever's religious/spiritual/philosophical background and current worldview 58
7. The griever's concurrent stressors. 58
8. The griever's family systems influences 59
9. The griever's participation in meaningful rituals. 59
10. Losses that tend to be stigmatized 60
How complicated grief presents 60
Absent or delayed grief. 61
Distorted grief. 61
Converted grief 62
Chronic grief. 62
PTSD in children and teens 63
The preschool subtype of PTSD 63

CHAPTER SEVEN:
Medical-model therapies as treatment 65
Psychological debriefing 65
Early cognitive-behavioral interventions 66
Short-term cognitive behavioral therapy 66
Evidence-based psychotherapy and grief 68
Drug therapy 69
EMDR 70
Psychosocial rehabilitation 70

CHAPTER EIGHT:
Mourning as "treatment" 73
Experience 75
Mourning Need 1: Acknowledge the reality of the losses 75
Primary and secondary losses in traumatic grief 76
Mourning Need 2: Feel the pain of the losses 77
Mourning Need 3: Remember the losses 79
Mourning Need 4: Develop a new self-identity 82
Complementary therapies for traumatic grief 82
Mourning Need 5: Search for meaning 83
Mourning Need 6: Receive ongoing support from others 85
A family-systems approach in PTSD 86
The importance of the six central needs of mourning 87

CHAPTER NINE:
The companioning philosophy of grief care 89
Advocating for the companioning model of grief care 92
Eleven tenets of companioning people in grief 94
A reminder about the art of empathy 95
Evasion-Encounter-Reconciliation 96

CHAPTER TEN:
When traumatic grief goes unmourned 101
Symptoms of carried grief 102
Difficulties with trust and intimacy 102
Depression and negative outlook 103
Anxiety and panic attacks 104

Psychic numbing and disconnection 104
Irritability and agitation 105
Substance abuse, addictions, eating disorders 105
Physical problems, real or imagined 106
Common life losses 107

CHAPTER ELEVEN:
Catch-up mourning for traumatic grief 109
A model for catch-up mourning 112
Step 1: Acknowledging carried grief 113
Step 2: Overcoming resistance to do the work 114
Step 3: Actively mourning carried grief 116
The needs of mourning in carried grief 118
Support groups and stories 121
Honoring our own stories 123
Step 4: Integrating carried grief 123

CHAPTER TWELVE:
Where to go from here? 127
Talk to your colleagues about the concept of PTSD as traumatic grief 128
Talk to the people in your care about their grief 128
Find ways to foster peer support 129
Integrate the six needs of mourning into your therapy programs 129
Integrate the concepts of carried grief and catch-up mourning into your therapy programs 130
Explore your own grief and mourning 130
Receive training in the companioning model of grief care 130

A FINAL WORD 133

"A culture that insists on seeing suffering as a pathology,
that is ashamed of suffering as a sign of failure or inadequacy,
a culture bent on the quick fix for emotional pain,
inevitably ends up denying both the
social and spiritual dimensions of our sorrows."

— MIRIAM GREENSPAN

Foreword

It was July of 2010 when a friend gave me a book to read, hoping that somehow it would help. It had only been three months since my beautiful wife, Carolyn, died in my arms. I returned to my military job just two weeks after her death. Somehow, I told myself, I needed to get over it and move on, just as I had with all of the losses in my life. Suck it up and get back to helping the warriors in the fleet and on the front lines. There were still wars going on, and I needed to do my part for the freedom of our country. Service above all and before self.

Little did I know that Carolyn's death would unlock a box of lifetime trauma and grief that I thought was securely sealed. But, as the weeks went by, I began to have feelings of fear, panic, depression, guilt, and loneliness—feelings that were so dark I had no idea what they were.

The book my friend gave me was still sitting on my nightstand. With all the courage I could muster, I picked it up and began to read *Understanding Your Grief.* That was all it took. That was my first introduction to Dr. Alan Wolfelt's work.

I discovered that one of Dr. Wolfelt's graduates from his Center for Loss and Life Transition, Marilyn, lived in our military community. Marilyn led a support group for those who had lost a loved one. With trepidation, I asked to join, and so began my first support group experience. It was during this time I began to understand Dr. Wolfelt's philosophy of "companioning" people in grief. I started to absorb his teaching that "you must mourn to heal" and the six needs of mourning. It was also during this time that my physicians suspected I may be struggling with post-traumatic stress disorder (PTSD).

In 2002 Carolyn and I had started a non-profit organization to help provide financial assistance to our most severely wounded veterans and the families of these veterans. Many thousands of our military were returning with severe physical injuries, and many more were returning with invisible injuries like PTSD. Our wounded warriors were overwhelming our country's ability to care for them. As far as mental health is concerned, that is still the case. In 2007 a U.S. senator asked that I testify to the President's Commission on Returning Wounded Warriors. In the testimony, I gave accounts of how our Veterans Affairs case managers, social workers, and mental health physicians were understaffed and ill trained to deal with the caseloads. While there has since been some improvement for our veterans, their mental health still goes under-"treated." PTSD is the most diagnosed and highest disability-rated mental health issue for our Iraq and Afghanistan veterans. Our system was looking for a quick fix in order to get them out the door.

With my suspected diagnosis of PTSD in late 2010, I pushed even harder to find a "cure" for myself. I was very fortunate to have mental- and physical-health physicians who were more centrist in their medical-model thinking and encouraged me to explore a more homeopathic approach to "treatment." That is when my search for a greater understanding of Dr. Wolfelt's holistic approach to grief began in earnest. Still, I believed I needed to get fixed quickly. It had already been six months. What was wrong with me?

In 2012 my foundation co-sponsored Dr. Wolfelt to present his companioning philosophy to our local community. After meeting Dr. Wolfelt and with the encouragement of family, friends, and doctors, I have attended many of his workshops at the Center for Loss and Life Transition in Fort Collins, Colorado. Very slowly I have come to know that there is no reward for speed. With Dr. Wolfelt's companioning, I have come to the understanding that grief from trauma is unique for each person. There is not a magic pill (much to my chagrin) to fix it. I have learned that traumatic grief, when not mourned, can become PTSD. Grief is complicated, messy, non-linear, and not scientific. I found myself fighting this new understanding of grief every step of the way. Where was science when I needed it? There are still days that I fight back and resist. I still push back on letting myself move into the deepest of the dark places, knowing that it will be painful.

I have always "stuffed" my grief or just sucked it up, from my earliest memories of my teenage friends taking their lives and my best friends not returning from war. I can remember Mike, John, Paul, and Cindy. I can remember the gun that Mike used to take his life. I can remember the bomb that killed Joe. But I had never mourned them, and they were my best friends. Carolyn's death started me on a journey that I never imagined and never wanted—a journey of going back so that I can go forward.

A diagnosis of PTSD brings with it a negative stigma. As former President George W. Bush stated in his PTSD message this last February, "Employers or potential employers do not want to take a chance on someone who has the PTSD label." President Bush is asking to have the "D" in PTSD" removed. "PTSD is an injury, not a disability," Bush said. Our Canadian friends have known this for some time. The Canadian Armed Forces, in 2001, started addressing PTSD as an injury referred to as "Operational Stress Injury." They started a program to help their veterans heal from their injury based on a peer-to-peer approach (companioning). This program has had tremendous success for their veterans.

Every day I receive phone calls and emails from an average of 10 veterans and their families who are pleading for help. One hundred percent of these veterans are diagnosed by the Veterans Administration as having PTSD, or what Dr. Wolfelt refers to in this book as "traumatic grief." Over the last 12 years our non-profit corporation has been honored to have supported thousands of veterans and tens of thousands of their family members. What I have discovered in this journey is that PTSD is not unique to the military. PTSD or traumatic grief is part of every culture and every country around the world.

But there is hope. I have found people who companion me. I have found a safe place to talk about my grief. I have found a safe place to mourn. I have started my soul work and spiritual work. Hope is now what I share with all I meet who are struggling with traumatic grief. Using the principles that Dr. Wolfelt lays out in this book, you will find the missing piece to helping those in your care heal the injury of traumatic grief.

My hope is that you as clinicians will consider incorporating Dr. Wolfelt's holistic philosophy into your practice. This book, *Reframing PTSD as Traumatic Grief*, is your guide. My traumatic grief journey is unique to me, but there are millions of us who are longing for a way back to a new normal. A way to find our new "divine spark" and with that, renewed joy, hope, and love. Please join us in this journey of helping others heal their traumatic grief.

Michael Cash
Founder/CEO Operation Family Fund
Program Manager, Naval Air Systems Command (Ret.)

Introduction

As I write this, my desk groans under the weight of stacks and stacks and more stacks of books on the diagnosis and treatment of post-traumatic stress disorder. Most are for counselors and caregivers—psychiatrists and psychologists and M.S.W.s and Ph.D.-types like me. As they should, they take the subject very seriously, citing a plethora of studies and hundreds of peer-reviewed journal articles. They are chockfull of meta-analyses and footnotes and indices and bibliographies. They approach PTSD with the utmost scientific rigor and in doing so, strive to physiologically and biochemically capture PTSD and elucidate the best methods with which to "fix" it.

> **"In our quest to contain and describe pathology, we have forgotten the philosophical roots of the field. The philosophers of ancient times took on no less of a goal than to better understand the whole of the human spirit, body, mind, and soul."**
>
> — TIAN DAYTON

This is not one of those books.

While the audience I hope to reach with this book and level of earnestness are the same, I seek to enter the arena of PTSD from a different doorway altogether. For more than 30 years, my area of interest—indeed, my passion—has been helping people understand the normal and necessary process we call grief. I began my formal start in this career by earning a Ph.D. in psychology and learning all the attendant rationales, methods, and conventions for diagnosing and treating mental health issues as illnesses.

Over the years, however, as I spent thousands of hours each year in the company of grievers and grief caregivers, counseling as well as speaking and teaching workshops, I came to understand that grief is not, after all, an illness or disease. Grief is what we think and feel inside when we lose something or someone we value. And since loss is a normal and unavoidable part of life, our response to loss is also normal. **Grief is love's conjoined twin. And if love is not an illness or diagnosis, then neither is grief.**

THE SOUL OF GRIEF

When I was a teenager I had a dream of creating a healing center where grief caregivers could come together and explore how we could be empowered to be agents of wholeness in the lives of grievers. I have taken that dream, clung to it, nurtured it, and never let it go. That dream, shaped by losses in my youth, ultimately transformed my life and has brought me tremendous meaning and joy.

In my twelve years of university-based training and in reading the available literature on grief counseling, I began to discover that our modern understanding of grief all too often lacks any appreciation for and attention to the spiritual, soul-based nature of the grief journey. As authors such as Frankl, Fromm, and Jung noted years ago (and Hillman and Moore more recently), academic psychology has been too interfaced with the natural sciences and laboratory methods of weighing, counting, and objective reporting.

Some of us, often through no fault of our own, but perhaps by the contamination of our formal training, have not seen the truth: that the journey into grief is a soul-based journey. We need to think about grief care differently than we now do. Because while our mission is certainly important, our current misunderstanding of loss and grief leads us astray.

I truly believe we are all here to, in part, contribute love and care to those our lives touch—each of us in his own way. Supporting my fellow human beings in grief nourishes my soul. If you are attempting to support people in grief from a place of open-heartedness and love, you are indeed nourishing your own soul and the souls of those you touch.

In professional caregiver circles, the companioning philosophy of grief care, which I explain in Chapter Ten of this book, has made me a "responsible rebel."

A responsible rebel is one who questions and challenges assumptive models. Rebels are not afraid to question established structures and forms. At the same time, rebels respect the rights of others to use different models of understanding, and provide leadership in ways that empower people rather than diminish them.

You see, I believe that at the very heart of grief lies an irreducible mystery. While I was trained in the medical model of mental health care, I have since come to discover that grief is a dimension of life experience that responds more appropriately to humbled souls. In this spirit, I invite you to open your heart to what follows.

When people come to me for support in grief, the soul is present. When they try as best they can to wrap words around their grief, trusting me with their vulnerability, I know we are meeting at a soul level. To look into the eyes of someone mourning a significant loss is to look into the window of the soul.

Soul really has to do with a sense of the heart being touched by feelings. An open heart that is grieving is a "well of reception"; it is moved entirely by what it has perceived. Soul also has to do with the overall journey of life as a story, as a representation of deep inner meaning. Soul is not a thing but a dimension of experiencing life and living. I see soul as the primary essence of our true nature, our spirit self, or our life force.

DE-PATHOLOGIZING PTSD

De-medicalizing grief has become a central part of my life's mission. If we can come to see grief as the natural and necessary process that it is, and if we can also learn to encourage and support one another in the expression of our grief, we can create a culture rich in compassion and self-fulfillment. We can foster hope and healing. We can, I believe, transform the life of human beings on Earth.

In recent years, as the diagnosis of PTSD has burgeoned and along with it, incidence and treatment studies as well as funding, media coverage, and general awareness, I have watched and listened with interest. While I am not—and do not pretend to be—a PTSD expert (actually, I have a bit of a problem with the concept of caregiving "expertise," but more on that later), I am more than an interested bystander. I am a grief educator and thought leader who has witnessed countless times, over the course of three decades, the profound harm done to grievers by a profession and culture that too often sees grief as disease and its symptoms as pathology. We are so uncomfortable with human suffering that we want to "treat" it away.

And so, I would now like to propose that post-traumatic stress is not a "disorder" but rather a component of normal, albeit complicated or traumatic, grief. We are able to integrate loss into our lives by calling it by its correct name—not labeling it as a disorder. This book explores this new way of thinking about PTSD and proposes a more holistic, de-pathologized model for its understanding and treatment—thus, the title *Reframing PTSD as Traumatic Grief.*

THE MISSING PIECE? MOURNING

After a discussion in Chapter One of the foundational principle that grief is not an illness but a natural and necessary response to loss, Chapter Two reviews types of traumatic loss and diagnostic criteria for PTSD. Chapter Three then compares the symptoms of PTSD to those of normal grief and proposes that instead of being categorized as a "disorder," post-traumatic stress be considered traumatic grief.

Next, Chapters Four and Five zoom in on the fear-related symptoms of first PTSD then normal grief, followed by a discussion in Chapter Six of traumatic grief as a kind of naturally complicated grief (because there are others).

Chapter Seven briefly summarizes a number of the most-used and –studied medical-model treatments for PTSD, including cognitive behavioral therapy and drug therapy, and raises questions about their true effectiveness when viewed through the lens of PTSD-as-traumatic-grief.

Chapters Eight and Nine, however, are the heart of this book. In them I emphasize that not medical treatment but instead mourning—the outward expression of grief—is the key to healing PTSD. If the current approach to treating PTSD is a jigsaw puzzle, mourning is the very large and important missing piece smack-dab in the center of the picture. You see, all who suffer significant loss grieve inside. This includes, of course, anyone affected by a traumatic event. To heal their grief, they must meet all six of what I call the central needs of mourning. While medical-model therapies (especially some kinds of psychotherapy, which is why they're effective to the extent they are) do help traumatized grievers begin to meet some or many of the central needs of mourning, none attempts to meet all six. Moreover, most medical-model treatments are too short-term and, even if and when they are helping traumatized grievers meet their mourning needs, have a strong propensity for teaching or implying to traumatized grievers that something is wrong with them. They convey to people with PTSD that they are sick or disordered and need to be cured.

What they need is companionship. Chapter Nine offers a different approach to caring for traumatized grievers—a method I call "companioning." A form of talk-therapy, companioning sees grief as normal and necessary, the traumatized griever himself as the only expert of his unique grief experience, and the counselor (whether professional or lay) as an empathetic companion.

Chapters Ten and Eleven go on to explore what happens when grief—normal or traumatic—is not sufficiently expressed, or mourned. I call this "carried grief." As I write this, many millions of traumatized grievers the world over are carrying grief. Some have received medical-model treatment and have been helped by it. Others have undergone these same treatments yet continue to suffer deeply. *Both groups*, I argue, are at risk for continuing symptoms of carried grief—such as difficulties with trust and intimacy, depression, anxiety, substance abuse, and others—until they are companioned through the process of fully mourning their carried grief. In other words, even when traumatized grievers receive medical treatment that eases or even eliminates their PTSD-diagnostic, fear-based symptoms, they are not "cured." Underneath the obvious symptoms lies an injured soul. And even when the obvious symptoms abate, the soul requires what I call "catch-up mourning." It is our responsibility as caregivers not to simply focus on immediate symptoms relief but to walk alongside traumatized grievers as, over time, they confront and find ways to express the true depth and breadth of their loss.

I realize that this book is more aptly shelved under Philosophy than How-to. But in Chapter Twelve, I do offer a number of possible next steps for medical-model-trained caregivers to integrate the understanding of PTSD as traumatic grief, the six central needs of mourning, and the companioning model of traumatic grief care into their practices. Mine is not an either/or proposition. Rather, it is a both/and proposition.

THANK YOU

If you are a caregiver accustomed to the medical model of PTSD diagnosis and treatment, I thank you for opening this book, and I encourage you to keep your mind—and more important, heart—open as you read its pages. I do not seek to deny or overturn evidence-based modes of inquiry and understanding. Rather, I seek to supplement them with what I believe to be a much-needed dose of appreciation for the fundamentally spiritual nature of the mysteries of human life and death. And I hope to influence you in ways that will result in more compassionate, empowering, and ennobling care for the millions of people affected by crippling traumatic grief each year.

You want to help people. That is why you became a mental health caregiver. I want the same thing. Let's work together to define and implement caregiving models that offer people with PTSD as well as our entire culture the best future.

Alan D. Wolfelt

Fort Collins, Colorado
August 2014

CHAPTER ONE

Grief not as an illness but as a response to injury

When we hear the word "grief," we tend to think of death. Grief is what we feel after someone we love dies. But this understanding of grief is far too narrow. **Actually, grief is what we think and feel whenever something we value is harmed or taken away.** And so, we grieve after divorce. We grieve when we are diagnosed with cancer. We grieve when our children grow up and move away. We grieve all the time, because life is replete with transitions and losses.

> "The pathology model makes the universal emotion of grief into a psychiatric problem."
>
> — MIRIAM GREENSPAN

When we experience a traumatic event, we also suffer losses. What those losses are depends on the circumstances of the event. We may lose someone we care about. We may lose some aspect of our health. We may lose our home or belongings. We may lose our trust in others. And we often lose our sense of safety and predictability in the world around us. This is to name just a few of the myriad losses that may make themselves known (consciously or subconsciously) in the aftermath of a traumatic event.

As with all loss, the many losses caused by a traumatic event naturally engender grief. We cannot help but grieve after a traumatic event. Everything we think and feel inside about the event, in fact, *is* our grief. In this book I talk a lot about grief, and it is this broader understanding of the word "grief" that I ask you to bring to bear on this chapter and all those that follow.

I myself became overtly aware of the concept of grief many years ago. As a teenager who had come to experience my own life losses, I set out to discover the principles that help people heal in grief. I earned a master's degree in psychology and then a doctorate. I completed my internship in clinical psychology at the Mayo Clinic. During these years, I also began to counsel bereaved families, so that I could learn up close from grievers and those who care for them.

To my dismay, I discovered that the majority of caregiving models for grief counselors were intertwined with the medical model of mental health care. They commonly portrayed grief as an illness that with proper assessment, diagnosis, and treatment can be cured. This paradigm dictates that we as caregivers, having studied and absorbed a body of knowledge and become experts, are responsible for "curing" our "patients." I beg to differ.

The language we use to describe the practice of grief support exposes our attitudes and beliefs about counseling as well as determines our practices. Because numerous historical roots of psychotherapy are deeply grounded in the medical model, because the medical model appears more scientific than other alternatives, and because the economics of practice are interfaced in a healthcare delivery system that requires diagnostic codes, the natural tendency has been to adopt medical-model language.

But as I familiarized myself with the nomenclature used in counseling people in grief, especially following death loss, I was taken aback: symptoms of pathology, disorders, diagnosis, and treatments. In my own search to learn so I could teach, I found that these more clinical, medical-model approaches have limitations that are profound and far-reaching.

At bottom, I discovered that our current models desperately needed what we could refer to as a "supplement of the soul." It seemed glaringly obvious to me that as fellow travelers in the journey into grief, we needed more life-giving, hope-filled models that incorporated not only the mind and body, but more important, the soul and the spirit. I found myself resonating more with the writings of people like Ram Dass, Stephen Levine, Victor Frankl, James Hillman, Thomas Moore, and Carl Jung.

Actually it was Carl Jung's writing that helped me understand that every psychological struggle is ultimately a matter of spirituality. In the end, when we as human beings mourn the many losses we encounter in life, we must (re)discover hope and meaning to go on living our tomorrows. Whether we like it or not, loss launches us on spiritual journeys of the heart and soul.

Our clinical understanding of grief all too often conveys that the end result of grief is a series of completed tasks and extinguished pain. I discovered that many mental health caregivers, in attempting to make a science of grief, had compartmentalized extremely complex emotions with neat clinical labels.

Our clinical understanding of grief all too often uses a "recovery" or "resolution" definition to suggest a return to "normalcy." Recovery, as understood by some grievers and caregivers alike, is erroneously seen as an absolute, a perfect state of re-establishment. We seem to want to go around any so-called "negative" moods and emotions quickly and efficiently. Yet, it occurred to me that if our role as caregivers is to first observe the soul as it is (a difficult task in many settings), then we need to abolish what I call the "resolution wish."

Our clinical understanding of grief for some is based on the model of crisis theory that purports that a person's life is in a state of homeostatic balance, then something "bad" comes along and knocks the person out of balance. Caregivers are taught intervention goals to reestablish the prior state of homeostasis and a return to "normal" functioning. There is only one major problem with this theory: it doesn't work. Why? Because a person's life is changed forever by significant loss. We are transformed by grief and do not return to prior states of "normal" based on interventions by outside forces.

Our clinical understanding of grief all too often pathologizes normal experiences. Traditional mental health care has focused the majority of attention on the diagnosis and treatment of pathologies, and in the quest for "fixes," little attention has been paid to the nature of emotional or spiritual health. As Dr. Martin Seligman, a former president of the American Psychological Association, observed, "The exclusive focus on pathology that has dominated so much of our discipline results in a model of the human being lacking the positive features that make life worth living."

Our clinical understanding of grief all too often privatizes grief as an isolated, individual experience. Mourning, by nature of its definition—"a shared social response to loss"—must be viewed in the broader context of social and family perspectives. (In fact, the person often perceived as "not doing well" in grief is usually the one who is trying to get help for the family system.)

Eventually, instead of thinking of grief as an illness, I came to understand it as a response to an injury that affects all aspects of our being—physical, cognitive, emotional, social, and spiritual. Loss is a psychic blow that often affects our bodies, our feelings, our relationships, our thoughts, and our very souls. And like a purely physical injury, the injury caused by loss must be examined and tended to for optimum healing to unfold.

What is the difference between an illness and an injury? Illness is an intrinsic, internal going-awry. It is a malfunction. It is a disorder. Injury, on the other hand, is the result of an external blow to an internal system. It is the effect of an outside action.

Grief is the response to an injury caused by loss. So, too, I believe, is post-traumatic stress.

TERMS USED IN THIS BOOK

You may notice that throughout this book I use or avoid a number of common terms. Instead of "patient" or "client," for example, I use the phrases "person experiencing PTSD" or "traumatized griever" because the former fly in the face of my core values and caregiving philosophy.

Client—literally, from the Latin for "obey" or "incline or bend"

Grief—the totality of what we think and feel inside after a loss

Griever—the person who has experienced a loss and has thoughts and feelings inside that stem from the loss

Mourning—the outward expression of the grief we experience inside

Patient—literally, "passive, long-term sufferer"

Treat—literally, "to drag"

"Words can inspire. And words can destroy. Choose yours well."

— ROBIN SHARMA

CHAPTER TWO

Traumatic loss and grief

Let us begin the discussion of post-traumatic stress with a brief but essential existential discussion.

Human beings, unique among living creatures in our level of self-awareness and time-independent consciousness, come to know—and, importantly, remember and try to make sense of—all manner of loss from an early age. We fall down and skin a knee. A dog snatches a cookie from our hands. Another child takes our toy. A grandparent dies. Slowly but inexorably, we become aware that we live in a world where loss is a part of everyday life.

> "A wound to the psycho-spiritual body can be just as crippling to the whole person as a wound to the body."
>
> — TIAN DAYTON

The grief we feel over each loss depends on our level of attachment. In other words, the more we are attached to someone or something, the more profound our grief when we lose that person or thing. (This is an oversimplification, as wished-for but unrealized attachment can also cause deep grief, but I hope you will allow me the generalization.) Losing a toy creates, of course, much less of a psychic injury than losing a grandparent.

So, the concept of attachments and the events that sever them is one way to think about loss. Another way is to take a look at Abraham Maslow's famous hierarchy of needs.

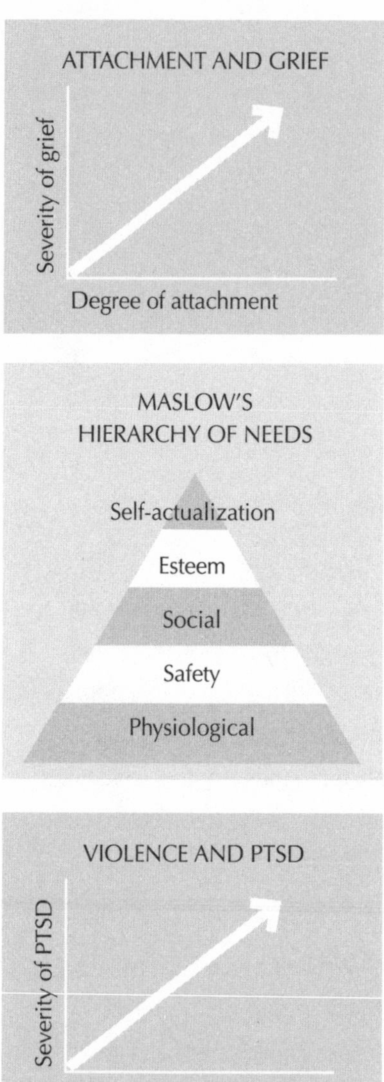

Events that injure our status quo, stability, or well-being in any of the slices of the pyramid are, in essence, losses. They are events that cause diminishments. Diminishment is loss, and vice versa.

So what happens if the loss results from trauma? If the event that causes the loss (in medical parlance, the "stressor") is violent and/or sudden and unexpected, when we are speaking of the loss in the vernacular we often conjure the term "traumatic." Experiencing a tornado up-close (a sudden and violent event) is traumatic. Being injured in a car crash (sudden and violent) is traumatic. Fighting in combat (violent and sometimes sudden) is traumatic. The death of a loved one to homicide (violent and sometimes, but not always, sudden) is traumatic.

In general, the more violent the loss experience, the more traumatic we consider it. This is one of the underlying assumptions of PTSD science.

Note that violent traumatic events first and foremost threaten the bottom two layers of Maslow's pyramid. They threaten or harm the bodies and the safety of us or those we care about. They activate the fight-or-flight fear response that is central to PTSD. But other loss events often impact our physical selves and our sense of safety, too. For example, if you are diagnosed with life-threatening or terminal cancer, even though you are not in imminent danger, both your body and your trust in the relative safety of your existence are suddenly and seriously injured. True, many violent traumatic events come and go quickly. A

WHICH LOSSES ARE TRAUMATIC?

	Violent	Non-Violent
Anticipated	I—*Menacing* Some military actions Prisoner of war Domestic abuse Cancer death (painful) Suicide (completed or attempted)	II—*Dreaded* Divorce Empty nest Cancer death (peaceful) Job loss Suicide (completed or attempted)
Sudden	III—*Horrific* Manslaughter Murder Natural disaster Military actions Car crash Rape Suicide (completed or attempted)	IV—*Out of the blue* Cardiac arrest Cancer diagnosis Divorce Unexpected death Job loss Suicide (completed or attempted)

tornado is upon us, and then it is gone. But is short duration an accurate criterion for trauma? I'm not convinced.

In thinking about which kinds of losses may be considered traumatic, I created this graph to demonstrate that teasing apart who may be considered traumatized by a loss event and who may not be is not at all a simple affair (more on that in the discussion on the next page of the DSM definition of PTSD). All of these losses may create profound grief. Many will cause numbness, intrusive thoughts, and anxiety, as well as a myriad of other symptoms. Moreover, in my counseling work, the people I have been honored to help have often taught me that more "garden-variety" losses, not listed on this chart (the expected death of an aged grandparent, for example), may also cause numbness, intrusive thoughts, and anxiety. We will next discuss PTSD in particular. For now, though, I simply want you to consider that **loss of any kind gives rise to a sometimes unpredictable but always complex array of grief symptoms that is likely impossible to objectively measure.**

WHAT IS PTSD?

Post-traumatic stress disorder, or PTSD, is the response to a serious psychological injury that is thought to affect an estimated eight percent of Americans at any given time—yielding a figure that today tops 25 million people. In recent decades it has risen to the fore as one of the most concerning and studied mental health issues because of its debilitating symptoms. It wasn't that long ago, however, that PTSD did not even have a name.

In the 20th century, the mental health field, like other disciplines, enjoyed an explosion of new theoretical and research-based understanding. These were the rich decades of Sigmund Freud (in his later career), B.F. Skinner, Jean Piaget, and Carl Rogers, among other luminaries. From our early 21st-century vantage point, it is sometimes easy to forget that most of our assumptions and canonical mental health knowledge are less than 100 years old.

While certainly human beings have experienced post-traumatic stress since the first human being walked the Earth, the term "post-traumatic stress disorder" did not appear in the *Diagnostic and Statistical Manual of Mental Disorders* until the DSM-III, in 1980 (after the Vietnam War). Before that, the anxiety provoked by various traumatic experiences was recognized in the DSM only in piecemeal fashion, including mentions of "shell shock" and "rape trauma syndrome."

After 1980, the definition of PTSD developed and evolved, both in professional diagnostic tools like the DSM and in a plethora of lay-friendly publications and websites.

Today, the website of the National Center for PTSD, which is a division of the U.S. Department of Veterans Affairs (the VA), explains PTSD to laypeople in this way:

> *After a trauma or life-threatening event, it is common to have reactions such as upsetting memories of the event, increased jumpiness, or trouble sleeping. If these reactions do not go away or if they get worse, you may have Posttraumatic Stress Disorder (PTSD).*

In turn, the website of the National Institute of Mental Health (NIMH) offers this lay-friendly explanation of PTSD:

> *When in danger, it's natural to feel afraid. This fear triggers many split-second*

PTSD BY THE NUMBERS

As our cultural and medical awareness of post-traumatic stress has grown, we've begun to realize the sheer magnitude of the issue. Here are some recent statistics.

- About six of every ten men and five of every ten women experience at least one trauma in their lives—in other words, about half of us.
- Although half of us experience a trauma, only about seven or eight percent of us ever have PTSD. So, about 15 percent of those who experience a trauma go on to develop PTSD.
- The types of traumas women are more likely to experience include sexual assault and child sexual abuse. Men are more likely to experience accidents, physical assault, combat, or disaster, or to witness death or injury.
- Women develop PTSD twice as often as men—10 percent of women versus five percent of men—possibly because they are more likely to be subject to interpersonal violence.
- In any given 12-month period in the United States, 3.5 percent of the population has PTSD. One-third of these people are said to have "severe" PTSD. That means that right this very minute, 11 million Americans have PTSD, and more than three million of them are considered to have severe PTSD.
- The average age of PTSD onset is 23 years old.

Sources: National Center for PTSD, NIMH, PTSD Alliance

changes in the body to prepare to defend against the danger or to avoid it. This 'fight or flight' response is a healthy reaction meant to protect a person from harm. But in post-traumatic stress disorder (PTSD), this reaction is changed or damaged. People who have PTSD may feel stresses or frightened even when they're no longer in danger.

PTSD develops after a terrifying ordeal that involved physical harm or the threat of physical harm. The person who develops PTSD may have been the one who was harmed, the harm may have happened to a loved one, or the person may have witnessed a harmful event that happened to loved ones or strangers.

PTSD was first brought to public attention in relation to war veterans, but it can result from a variety of traumatic incidents, such as mugging, rape, torture, being kidnapped or held captive, child abuse, car accidents, train wrecks, plane crashes, bombings, or natural disasters such as floods or earthquakes.

Note that both the National Center for PTSD and the NIMH appear to limit PTSD to people who have personally been affected by physically dangerous events.

In the past, the *Diagnostic and Statistical Manual* classified PTSD among anxiety disorders. Today the DSM-5 has moved PTSD to a new category called "trauma- and stressor-related disorders."

THE INCITING EVENT, OR "STRESSOR"

Since the DSM-III, what counts as a "recognizable stressor" has been examined and defined and redefined. The current DSM, the DSM-5, stipulates that a PTSD diagnosis can only be made if the person was exposed to death, threatened death, actual or threatened serious injury, or actual or threatened sexual violence, as follows (criterion A):

1. Direct exposure
2. Witnessing, in person
3. Indirectly, by learning that a close relative or close friend was exposed to trauma. If the event involved actual or threatened death, it must have been violent or accidental.
4. Repeated or extreme indirect exposure to aversive details of the event(s), usually in the course of professional duties (e.g., first responders, collecting body parts; professionals repeatedly exposed to details of child abuse). This does not include indirect nonprofessional exposure through electronic media, television, movies, or pictures.

So, given this definition of the kinds of experiences that cause PTSD, what's included? Violent acts of war or terrorism, certainly. Many murders and suicides. Natural disasters. Sexual assault. Violent accidents, such as car crashes. I think we all agree that exposure to these experiences—whether by direct exposure, witnessing, or learning of a loved one's involvement—is traumatic and can give rise to the debilitating symptoms outlined in Chapter Three.

But what may be reasonably excluded under this definition also merits consideration. According to at least one possible interpretation of this definition, if your son attempts suicide by taking too many sleeping pills (a nonviolent act) but is not successful, and you do not witness it but later find out about it, you cannot technically develop PTSD—even if you end up having intrusive thoughts, numbness, anxiety, and even nightmares about this difficult reality. Similarly, if you learn that your partner of many years has been sexually abusing children, you cannot go on to have PTSD. And if you receive a phone call in the middle of the night saying that your fit, healthy, and young best friend died of a sudden stroke, you cannot develop PTSD. Does this make sense? Maybe or maybe not. **Again, I would simply urge readers of this book to consider that common circumstances yield highly individualized grief responses that are not easily placed in a box.**

INCITING EVENTS IN PTSD

Following is a list of traumatic events that, it is generally agreed, may give rise to PTSD. And although I use the term "traumatic event" throughout this book, the stressor may be a single event or repeated exposure. Also, it may be experienced directly, witnessed, or experienced by a loved one.

Mass trauma (e.g., plane crash)

Terrorist attack (e.g. 9/11)

Rape or sexual abuse

Physical abuse

Combat

Natural disasters

Serious accidents

Captivity

Sudden death

Of course, not everyone agrees with the DSM's language about what constitutes a traumatic event. In fact, in 2013 the NIMH decided to eschew the DSM and instead develop its own diagnostic criteria not just for PTSD but for all mental health issues. And my chart of traumatic losses on page 17 may serve to demonstrate that loss, and the resulting grief, comes in many shades of gray.

Through this discussion of the inciting event, or the "stressor," I do not mean to be disrespectful or trivialize a very real psychic injury. Neither do I necessarily seek a redefinition of PTSD in the next DSM. Rather, I merely hope to shine a light on the fact that **when we medicalize and attempt to strictly define and measure an emotional and spiritual internal response to an external reality, we sometimes end up missing the point.** My purpose is to join in the conversation about this important topic—to reframe it, not to determine how it should come out.

PTSD AND THE MILITARY

While it studies and provides assistance for traumas from all sources, the National Center for PTSD is a program of the VA. That alone tells you how significant an issue PTSD is in the military today.

According to the Center's website, PTSD occurs in about 11 to 20 percent of veterans of the wars in Iraq and Afghanistan, as many as 10 percent of Gulf War vets, and fully 30 percent of Vietnam vets. (Other VA studies indicate that these percentages may actually be much higher.) Soldiers with multiple deployments are more likely to experience PTSD.

In addition to combat-related trauma, many military personnel experience sexual trauma while serving for their country. Fully 23 percent of women reported sexual assault while in the military, and 55 percent of women and 38 percent of men have experienced sexual harassment while in the military.

What's more, about seven percent of combat veterans experience both traumatic brain injury and PTSD concurrently. And an estimated 8,000 U.S. veterans die each year by suicide.

All told, millions of U.S. military veterans suffer from PTSD, and it is their suffering that has brought PTSD in general into the national spotlight. According to a RAND study, only half of them seek treatment, and of the half that seek treatment, only half get "minimally adequate" treatment.

The gross inadequacy of care for military veterans with PTSD is one of the main reasons I wrote this book. Today, as I ready it for press, the VA is under massive criticism for its substandard and untimely care in general. The good news is that at least some government funding has finally been allocated to PTSD care. The bad news is that the purse strings are in the hands of an organization that institutionalizes the medical model of mental health care as well as a culture of violence, a stoic machismo, a dearth of spirituality, and a cookie-cutter approach to everything.

Our veterans deserve better. Their souls are deeply wounded, and only a holistic approach to their care will help them truly heal.

PTSD SUB-TYPES

DISSOCIATIVE

In dissociative PTSD, the person sees the traumatic event as unreal, as a dream, or as somehow apart from him. People in grief often experience some degree of dissociative symptoms as well, especially in cases of unexpected loss (quadrants III and IV in the chart on page 17).

DELAYED

Delayed PTSD is PTSD that cannot be fully diagnosed until six months (or later) following the traumatic event, even if some symptoms were present before that. I would note that it's common for grief to slowly bloom and that it almost always gets worse before it gets better.

PARTIAL

While this sub-type was not included in the DSM-5, it is still used as a diagnostic category (formally or informally) in research and in practice. People with partial PTSD meet some but not all of the criteria required for a PTSD diagnosis. Of course, I believe that any symptoms of psychic injury following a significant loss, whether traumatic or non-traumatic, are care-eliciting symptoms (see page 34). The very concept of "partial PTSD," in fact, is evidence that attempts to measure and medicalize often do not jibe with the normal and natural messiness of the human soul.

SECONDARY

While secondary PTSD is not formally a sub-type (using the DSM-5 as the bible), it is a common experience among family members of people with PTSD. People who live with and care for someone with PTSD begin to anticipate the expression of PTSD symptoms or "episodes." They often take on symptoms of PTSD themselves, such as negativity and anxiety.

In essence, those affected by secondary PTSD are struggling to help the person with PTSD cope even as they are struggling with their own internal grief over the fact that a loved one suffers traumatic grief. In my experience, a family-systems counseling approach is the best way to help both the primary person with PTSD and her family (see page 86).

PRESCHOOL

See PTSD in Children and Teens, page 63.

CHAPTER THREE

The symptoms of PTSD and traumatic grief

Regardless of your belief in and reliance on clear-cut diagnoses, mental health clinicians must always work to understand each person's symptoms. After all, it is the symptoms, not the diagnosis, from which they seek relief and for which I urge a new understanding.

> "The power of emotions as a profound way of knowing and healing is barely recognized in a society that worships science and more masculine forms of knowing."
>
> — MIRIAM GREENSPAN

PTSD SYMPTOMS

In the case of PTSD, the primary symptoms involve the re-experiencing or repeated intrusion of the event, including a) thoughts or perception, b) images, c) dreams, d) illusions or hallucinations, e) dissociative flashbacks, and/or f) psychological and physiological reactions to cues that remind the person of the event. The DSM-5 says that at least one of these things must be persistently occurring (criterion B).

The remaining symptoms involve avoidance, negative cognition and mood, and hyper-arousal.

Avoidance is essential to the diagnosis. People who avoid thoughts, feelings, or conversations about the event OR activities, places, or other people that remind them of the event are considered to be exhibiting avoidance. The DSM-5 says one of these must be present (criterion C).

Negative alteration in cognition and mood can include an inability to remember significant aspects of the event; persistent and exaggerated negative beliefs about oneself, others, and the world; persistent, distorted thoughts about the cause or consequences of the event; persistent negativity; markedly diminished interest or participation in significant activities; feelings of detachment or estrangement from others; and/or a persistent inability to experience positive emotions. The DSM-5 says two or more of these symptoms must be present (criterion D).

Hyper-arousal symptoms are those we think of as being connected to fear and fight-or-flight: difficulty sleeping; irritability or aggressive behavior; self-destructive or reckless behavior; difficulty concentrating; hyper-vigilance; and exaggerated startle response. At least two of these must be present, according to the DSM-5 (criterion E).

Finally, to meet the DSM-5 definition of PTSD the symptoms (B, C, D, and E) must have been present for at least a month and must also be causing significant distress or functional impairment.

UNCOMPLICATED GRIEF SYMPTOMS

Now let's take a look at common symptoms of grief.

Normal, uncomplicated grief is a conglomeration of ever-changing thoughts and feelings that stem from loss. I will briefly list the most common symptoms below as a means of furthering our discussion of post-traumatic stress as a form of grief.

Shock, numbness, denial, and disbelief

"It feels like a dream," people in early grief often say. "I feel like I might wake up and none of this will have happened." They also say, "I was there, but yet I really wasn't. I managed to do what needed to be done, but I didn't feel a part of it."

Shock, numbness, and disbelief are nature's way of temporarily protecting grievers from the full reality of a loss. Much as physical shock shuts extraneous bodily functions down so that vital operations can be maintained, emotional shock helps insulate people psychologically until they are more able to tolerate what they don't want to believe.

This mixture of shock, numbness, and disbelief acts as an anesthetic: the pain exists, but grievers may not experience it fully. Typically, a physiological component also accompanies feelings of shock. The autonomic nervous system is affected and may cause heart palpitations, queasiness, stomach pain, and dizziness.

Disorganization, confusion, searching, and yearning

Perhaps the most isolating and frightening part of the journey through grief is the sense of disorganization, confusion, searching, and yearning that often comes with the loss. These feelings frequently arise when the griever begins to be confronted with the reality of the loss.

People express disorganization and confusion in their inability to complete tasks. They may start to do something but never finish. They may feel forgetful and ineffective, especially early in the morning and late at night, when fatigue and lethargy are most prominent.

When someone loved has died, they may experience a restless searching for the person. Yearning and preoccupation with memories can leave grievers feeling drained. They can even experience a shift in perception: other people may begin to look like the person who died.

Other common, related experiences include difficulties eating and sleeping. Grievers may experience a loss of appetite or find themselves overeating. Even when they do eat, they may be unable to taste the food. Having trouble falling asleep and early morning awakening are also common experiences associated with this dimension of grief.

Anxiety, panic, and fear

Feelings of anxiety, panic, and fear are common components of the grief experience. Grievers ask themselves, "Am I going to be OK? Will I survive this?" These questions are natural. The grievers' sense of security has been threatened, so they are naturally anxious.

A variety of thoughts and situations can increase anxiety, panic, and fear. For example, grievers may be afraid of what the future holds or that they will experience other losses. They may be more aware of their own vulnerability or mortality, which can be scary. They may feel vulnerable, even unable to survive. They may feel panicky about their inability to concentrate. Financial problems can compound feelings of anxiety.

Anxiety and depression often go hand-in-hand. In fact, surveys show that 60 to 70 percent of people with depression also have anxiety, and half of people with anxiety also have significant depression. They are now thought by many mental health caregivers to be two faces of one symptom.

Explosive emotions

Anger, hate, blame, terror, resentment, rage, and jealousy are explosive, volatile, yet natural parts of the grief journey. It helps to understand that all these feelings are, at bottom, a form of protest. Think of the toddler whose favorite toy is yanked out of his hands. This toddler wants the toy; when it's taken, his instinctive reaction may be to scream or cry or hit. When someone or something you care about is taken from you, your instinctive reaction may be much the same.

Explosive emotions may surface at any time during the grief journey. Grievers may direct these emotions at a person who died or left (such as in divorce), at the organization that caused the loss (such as a job lay-off), at friends and family members, at doctors, at people who haven't experienced loss, at God.

People sometimes oversimplify explosive emotions by looking only at anger. Actually, grievers may experience a whole range of intense feelings such as those listed above. Underneath these emotions are usually feelings of pain, helplessness, fear, hurt, and frustration.

Guilt and regret

Guilt, regret, and self-blame are common and natural feelings after a loss. Grievers often have a case of the "if-onlys": If only I had gotten him to the doctor sooner… If only I had been more kind… If only I hadn't said…

Other potential aspects of guilt and regret, particularly after a death, include

- *Survivor guilt* - Sometimes being alive when someone they love has died can foster survivor guilt in grievers.

- *Relief-guilt* - Grievers naturally feel relief if someone they love dies after a long period of illness and suffering. But feelings of relief can also make them feel guilty. "I shouldn't be feeling relieved," they may think.

- *Joy-guilt* - Like relief-guilt, joy-guilt is about thinking that happy feelings are bad at a time of loss. One day grievers might find themselves smiling or laughing at something, only to chastise themselves for having felt happy for a minute.

Sadness and depression

Grievers often describe sadness as the most painful feeling on the journey through grief. Even in normal, uncomplicated grief, it often takes weeks or months after the loss event before grievers arrive at the full depth of their sorrow. Relatedly, depression and its attendant anhedonia—literally, "without pleasure"—are also extremely common in grief.

Relief

In normal grief, feelings of relief and release are common, especially when the loss includes some element of "it's finally over." If you are laid off or fired from a job that you needed for the paycheck but hated, you will probably feel relief as well as other symptoms of grief. If someone dies who in life abused you, you may well feel a sense of relief. The expression of normal grief thoughts and feelings also commonly causes feelings of relief and release. "I feel so much better now that I've said that," people often say to me.

"COMORBIDITIES" IN PTSD

As you know, people who have PTSD often present with other significant issues as well. To my way of thinking, all of the symptoms, especially those that arose after the traumatic event, can be considered part of the grief response. Those that predate the traumatic event may be separate challenges or, often, components and symptoms of carried grief (see chapter Ten).

Also, I can't help but mention here that the term "comorbidity" means concurrent illness or disease. It's terminology like this—and the attendant thinking—that has led to the pathologizing of grief symptoms.

SLEEP PROBLEMS

The hyper-arousal of PTSD often causes sleep disturbances, as do the negative thoughts (worry) and the not-uncommon nightmares. As we reminded ourselves by reviewing Maslow's pyramid, the physical needs of the body, including sleep, must be tended to before any higher-order work can be done. Sleep problems in normal grief are also common.

DEPRESSION

PTSD and deep depression often go hand-in-hand. People who were depressed before the traumatic event are at greater risk for PTSD, and depression can also be seen as a symptom of grief following a traumatic event. I think it's virtually impossible, and kind of beside the point, to tease apart depression and PTSD. But people whose depression is pronounced may need antidepressant therapy as one component of their care. (Some people refuse antidepressants because of the distressing side effects or the perceived stigma of taking drugs for a "mental illness." Like over-prescribing antidepressants, under-utilization can also be a challenge.)

SUBSTANCE ABUSE

People with mental health challenges often self-treat with alcohol and drugs, including people in grief. You hurt so you seek to dull your pain, but of course, alcohol and drugs only make things worse. Concurrent substance-abuse treatment alongside PTSD therapies may be necessary to help these people.

TRAUMATIC BRAIN INJURY

Many military veterans as well as people who have experienced violent accidents and natural disasters have PTSD and traumatic brain injury (TBI). In other words, in addition to a psychic injury to the brain, this subset of people with PTSD has also suffered a physical injury to the brain, which compounds common PTSD symptoms and also creates additional symptoms. These people require and deserve well-coordinated care among medical and mental health caregivers. From a grief standpoint, they need an extra layer of compassionate understanding and more time and latitude to heal.

SUICIDE RISK

Childhood abuse, sexual trauma, combat trauma, and other forms of trauma heighten the risk of suicide. In general, people with PTSD are at higher risk for suicide. Caregivers like you are typically well-trained to assess suicidal impulses and take appropriate action. I do believe that the "there's something wrong with you" medical-model understanding of PTSD contributes to the shaming and stigma that sometimes precipitates suicide. Also, there's no doubt that PTSD is a contributing factor in many of the 22-plus suicides per day among U.S. military veterans.

PTSD VERSUS GRIEF

We've reviewed the DSM-required symptoms for a PTSD diagnosis, and I've listed the most common symptoms of normal, uncomplicated grief that I have witnessed or that have been described to me in my nearly four decades as a grief counselor and educator.

Let's consider them side-by-side in this chart:

SYMPTOM	PTSD	NORMAL GRIEF
Thoughts or perception about the event/loss	✔	✔
Images of the event/loss	✔	✔
Dreams about the event/loss	✔	✔
Illusions or hallucinations	✔	✔
Dissociative flashbacks	✔	Sometimes
Psychological or physical reactions to cues	✔	✔
An inability to remember significant aspects of the event	✔	Sometimes
Avoiding thoughts, feelings, conversations, places, or people that are reminders	✔	✔
Persistent and negative beliefs about self, others, or world	✔	Sometimes
Persistent, distorted thoughts about the cause or consequences of the event/loss	✔	Sometimes
Persistent negativity	✔	Sometimes
Markedly diminished interest or participation in significant activities	✔	✔
Feelings of detachment or estrangement from others; self-isolating behavior	✔	✔
Persistent inability to experience positive emotions; anhedonia	✔	✔
Difficulty sleeping	✔	✔
Irritability or anger outbursts; explosive emotions	✔	✔
Difficulty concentrating; disorganization, confusion	✔	✔
Hyper-vigilance	✔	Sometimes
Exaggerated startle response; anxiety, panic, fear	✔	✔

Though this chart does not attempt to capture the nuanced differences between typical PTSD symptoms and normal grief, such as *degree* or *duration* of irritability or hallucinations, for example, it does, at a glance, tell us that perhaps the two injury responses have a lot in common.

If we were to illustrate this as a Venn diagram, it might look something like this:

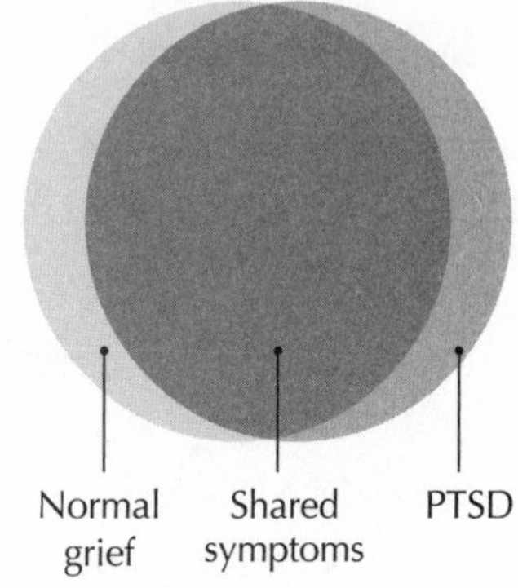

In essence, the fear-response symptoms (more on that in the next chapter) are often more prominent in PTSD, but otherwise, they can and sometimes do look and sound almost exactly alike.

TRAUMATIC GRIEF

So far we have explored the (gray) definitions of traumatic loss and reviewed the symptoms of PTSD and normal grief. Now let's consider what happens when we view PTSD through the lens of grief.

I write many books about grief and mourning for laypeople because it's my passionate belief that when they are suffering in the aftermath of a loss, people in our mourning-avoidant culture, especially, need help understanding that all the thoughts and feelings they are experiencing inside are not only normal but necessary. They also need encouragement to take the essential second step of expressing all those thoughts and feelings—in other words, mourning.

One of the books I wrote some years ago is entitled *Healing Your Traumatized Heart: 100 Practical Ideas After Someone You Love Dies a Sudden, Violent Death.* In that short, practical resource, I offered compassionate understanding and guidance to those grieving a death caused by a homicide, suicide, or accident. More recently I wrote a similar book for people who have been traumatized by a natural disaster.

In the first book, I defined "trauma" as any event of such intensity, brutality, or magnitude of horror that it would overwhelm any human being's capacity to cope. I went on to explain to its readers that after a traumatic loss, it is normal and necessary to replay and reconsider over and over the circumstances of the death. "Such replay helps you begin to acknowledge the reality of the death and integrate it into your life," I wrote. "It is as if your mind needs to devote time and energy to comprehending the circumstances of the death before it can move on to confronting the fact that someone you love has died and will never be present to you again.

"The traumatic nature of the death and your thoughts and feelings about it will color every aspect of your grief," I went on. "It is part of your grief. But it is not the totality of your grief. Other factors that contribute to your grief include the nature of the relationship you had with the person who died, your unique personality, your religious and cultural backgrounds, your gender, your age, your previous experiences with loss, as well as others. Your grief is a complicated blend of thoughts and emotions, most of which stem from your love for the person who died. Over time you will come to find that your grief is as much or more about the life as it is about the death."

I went on to define PTSD and explained that many people who have experienced the death of a loved one to homicide, suicide, or accidental death are traumatized without developing full-blown PTSD. They almost always replay or re-imagine the event. They experience psychic numbing, which is a form of heightened shock, a normal response to an abnormal event. They are anxious and often angry. "But if you are still able to function in your daily life and interact lovingly with others," I wrote, "you may not meet the technical criteria for PTSD. Still, you are in need of special care and consideration, both from yourself and others."

Embedded in these paragraphs are the three main rules of thumb I share with laypeople whose loss experience was traumatic—lessons I learned from many of them in the first place:

1. The traumatic nature of the loss creates a unique, two-part grief experience: one focused on the event itself and one focused on the losses the event created.
2. If you are still able to function in your daily life and interact lovingly with others, you may not need professional help for PTSD.
3. Even if you may not need professional help for PTSD, traumatic loss often gives rise to a complicated grief response, and people suffering from traumatic grief need special care and consideration.

In short, I would say that traumatic grief and what is called PTSD are part of the same continuum, with PTSD inhabiting the extreme far end of the bell curve. Further, I would suggest that the label "post-traumatic stress disorder" implies an illness where actually there is what is a normal (albeit stuck) response to an abnormally severe injury. The term "disorder" is frightening and seems permanent. It perpetuates the stigma. The concept of injury, on the other hand, implies that the symptoms are something that, with appropriate attention, can and will heal. Injury is more hopeful.

I propose that the term "traumatic grief" actually captures better than the term "PTSD" the totality of people's experience following traumatic loss. "PTSD" is all about the event of the loss, whereas "traumatic grief" acknowledges both the traumatic event and the entirety of the grief journey that ensues. Focusing on PTSD to the exclusion of grief is like performing a triple-bypass on a person with coronary artery disease without also counseling him about diet and exercise and working closely with him through a course of cardiac rehab. Yes, you may "fix" the immediate, life-threatening symptoms, but you don't really improve his health or well-being.

CARE-ELICITING SYMPTOMS

Symptoms that reveal the presence of something—in this case, an injury—that needs and deserves attention.

Fundamentally, the symptoms of grief, normal or traumatic, are care-eliciting symptoms. They are not signs of illness but rather symptoms of an injury that needs careful and compassionate tending. And the sort of tending they most need is the subject of the later chapters of this book.

As a clinician who has counseled many people in grief over the last four decades, I am well aware of the utility and exigencies of diagnostic codes and "labels." In our current health-care climate, to be diagnosed with PTSD or another mental illness is to open the doorway to treatment. If a diagnostic code isn't rendered, insurance-company reimbursement isn't triggered. And most people do not have the resources to pay for ongoing therapy or treatment on their own. (As an aside, I also feel the need to mention the concurrent abuse of the PTSD diagnosis thought to be happening right now in the U.S. military. Today, veterans with PTSD can receive up to $3,000 a month in disability payments, which has led, naturally, to PTSD "faking" and fraud. It's disgraceful that resources so desperately needed for the care of traumatized grievers could be compromised by this development.)

Moreover, the label "PTSD" is in essence a handle that allows our culture and our caregivers to grab hold of the issue. We are witnessing the brokenness of millions of our friends, neighbors, and people in our care, so we create a shorthand term that enables us to talk to one another about what we are seeing.

So, perhaps for now, at least, diagnoses and terms like PTSD serve an essential purpose.

Still, I also believe that our current medical focus on PTSD, while in some ways warranted and appropriate, inures us to the fact that **grief itself, in all its many shades and variations, is the overarching public health issue that merits acknowledgment, resources, and study.** What about the many millions suffering emotionally and spiritually today in the wake of Alzheimer's disease, cancer, poverty, emotional abuse, and/or non-traumatic death, to name just a few other public health issues? PTSD is important. But as with our person with cardiac trouble, overall wellness should always be the highest-level goal.

PTSD VERSUS OPERATIONAL STRESS INJURY

The Canadian military uses the phrase "operational stress injury," or OSI, to describe "any persistent psychological difficulty resulting from operational duties performed while serving in the Canadian Armed Forces or as a member of the Royal Canadian Mounted Police." This includes PTSD as well as anxiety disorders, depression, and other symptoms that are less severe but still interfere with daily functioning.

I like the OSI term because it more broadly recognizes care-eliciting symptoms and doesn't require, as the DSM does, that certain criteria be met or that a certain diagnostic label be applied. If you have symptoms, especially if they are interfering with your day-to-day life, that means you need and deserve help. That is as it should be.

CHAPTER FOUR

The fear factor of PTSD

At the heart of the current PTSD crisis is the traumatic griever's fear response.

> "PTSD is the fear controlling you. Exposing your fear is controlling your PTSD."
>
> — ANTHONY PARSONS

When we are under imminent threat, our ancient fight-or-flight system kicks in. This is the evolutionary, biological wiring that in dangerous situations serves to keep us alive.

If I suddenly notice that a predator—a grizzly bear, say—is nearby and is approaching me, my brain recognizes "Danger!" and activates my sympathetic nervous system and my adrenal-corticol system, setting a cascade of physical responses in motion. My sympathetic nervous system uses nerve pathways in my body to initiate reactions, while my adrenal-corticol system releases hormones through the bloodstream.

My brain's amygdalae, two small clusters of cells deep in my temporal lobes that are in charge of emotional processing, interpret what I am seeing as danger and instantly send a distress signal to my hypothalamus. My hypothalamus is my stress command center, in charge of my autonomic nervous system. It reaches out to my adrenal glands, which pump out epinephrine, a.k.a. adrenaline.

My heart rate increases, pushing blood to my muscles, heart, and other vital organs.

My breathing rate increases so I can take in more oxygen.

My digestion slows down or stops, because it's not necessary right now.

My blood vessels constrict to channel blood to my muscles.

My pupils dilate so I can see better.

My brain receives the extra oxygen and goes into hyper-alert status.

In short, my body prepares to either run away or stay and fight.

After the initial surge of adrenaline subsides, if I am still seeing that scary grizzly bear (instead of realizing at this point that what I saw was just a bear-shaped shadow), my hypothalamus activates what is known as the HPA (hypothalamic-pituitary-adrenal) axis. This second punch in the one-two punch stress response *keeps* my body in hyper-alert mode. My pituitary releases a hormone called *adrenocorticotropic hormone*, or ACTH, which travels to my adrenal glands, prompting them to release cortisol. Also called "the stress hormone," cortisol maintains my body's fluid balance and blood pressure and checks non-essential bodily functions, such as reproductive drive, immunity, and growth.

All of this (and more) happens without my conscious awareness or permission. Instead, my body's reaction to danger is subconscious and primal. The name that we use to describe what my body is feeling is "fear." I see danger, so I feel fear. In other words, fear is what it feels like in my body when my body's primal fight-or-flight system has been activated.

For millennia, fear has kept us alive. When we are in true physical danger, it still does. You'd better believe that if I encounter a grizzly bear on my next hike in the northern Rocky Mountains, I'll be grateful for fear. But now that human societies and technologies have evolved to the point that in our daily lives we rarely experience imminent life-or-death situations, our fear response is more likely to take up residence as chronic worry and anxiety.

PTSD AND THE BRAIN

As you may know, the new science of PTSD has determined that the fight-or-flight system that activates when we experience a traumatic event can essentially become stuck. If I survive a close call with a tornado, for example, it is my fight-or-flight system that may have propelled me to the basement. As the tornado passed overhead and I experienced the terror of the sounds and sensations of horrific winds, flying debris, and collapsing structures—as well as, possibly, injury or the death of others—naturally I continue to feel fear and remain in fight-or-flight mode.

But after the tornado is long gone, in the weeks and months after the experience, if I still feel numb and anxious and can't seem to shake the intrusive, horrific memories of what it was like to live through the horror of this natural disaster, I may be diagnosed with PTSD.

Developments in technology in the last 20 or so years, especially functional MRIs, have allowed researchers to image the brains of people affected by PTSD. One finding has been that people with PTSD have much more spontaneous brain activity in their amygdalae. In other words, even when they are in a totally safe and quiet environment, people with PTSD have amygdalae that are still found to be firing. In addition, even in people whose PTSD symptoms have abated, the amygdala has been found to be smaller in volume.

Another lingering brain effect of PTSD seems to reside in the brain's hippocampi, which lie next to the amygdalae and are the center of memory storage and recall. While the amygdala detects threats, the hippocampus links the fear response to the context in which the threat is happening. Some studies indicate that, like the amygdala, the hippocampus shrinks after a traumatic event, possibly due to an overdose of cortisol. It is thought that the damaged hippocampi may prevent flashbacks and nightmares from being properly processed and/or may cause difficulty recalling parts of the traumatic event. You might think of the injured hippocampus as a glitchy hard drive.

It is also thought that the HPA axis may become chronically disrupted in PTSD. Studies of children who lost a parent in the September 11, 2001, terrorist attacks, for example, showed persistent HPA axis dysregulation in the form of continuously elevated cortisol levels two years after the event.

A "DISEASE" OF MEMORY

PTSD is sometimes referred to as a disease of memory. In an article by J. Douglas Bremmer, M.D., of Yale University School of Medicine and the National Center for PTSD, the author explains that victims of childhood abuse often have troubles with declarative memory (remembering facts) and atypical gaps in memory that span minutes or days.

IS PTSD AN INHERITED PREDISPOSITION?

Not everyone who experiences the same traumatic event develops PTSD. While I would argue that everyone who experiences a traumatic event must mourn their unique grief, and that what that grief looks and feels like for different people will vary along a continuum, it's true that some people have more profound and intransigent grief responses. Could it be genetic?

Some brain research suggests that people most susceptible to PTSD have neurological anomalies in their brains that may be inherited. One study, by Lisa Shin of Tufts University, for example, showed that in people with PTSD, the amygdala is hyperactive, while the medial prefrontal cortex, which dampens stress, is underactive.

Her research also implies that the kind of treatment that will be most effective in helping a PTSD sufferer may depend on his biology. "So far we are finding that people with a more highly activated medial prefrontal cortex do better in exposure therapy, and those who had a hyperactive amygdala do worse," said Shin in a 2011 article.

Other research has indicated that two genes involved in serotonin production are linked to a higher susceptibility to PTSD. People with genetically lower production of serotonin were found to be more likely to develop PTSD than other experiencers of the same trauma.

Perhaps neurological and genetics testing will one day be an inexpensive and standard part of an initial PTSD assessment, and maybe these findings will help us more readily help those who come to us. If so, I welcome these developments. But will physical findings ever replace the need for compassionate emotional and spiritual grief support following a trauma? Absolutely not.

After studying the brains of childhood abuse victims and comparing them to the brains of Vietnam combat veterans, he and his team concluded that trauma causes measurable physical changes to the brain's hippocampus as well as the medial prefrontal cortex. These changes, the researchers believe, are what lead not only to classic PTSD symptoms (such as the psychological fear response to cues that remind the person of the trauma event and selective amnesia of the trauma event) but also future, seemingly unrelated memory problems (such as difficulty learning and remembering new information).

Here in the first quarter of the twenty-first century, the brain is still largely a mystery, and researchers are just beginning to identify and understand the biological basis of PTSD. It is unclear at this point, for example, whether smaller amygdalae and hippocampi are the *result* of PTSD or instead, perhaps, the *cause* of PTSD.

CAN—AND SHOULD—WE *PREVENT* TRAUMATIC MEMORIES?

To me it sounds like something out of a dystopian sci-fi film, but it's real: scientists are looking at ways to prevent PTSD with an injection.

Researchers at Emory University have been injecting mice with an experimental agent called SR-8993 immediately following a traumatic event, which involved "a single traumatic exposure to immobilization stress." The agent targets the opioid-receptor-like 1 gene, OPRL1.

Without the injection, the traumatized mice showed impairment in long-term declarative memory as well as prolonged anxiety and deficits in spatial learning. With the injection, the traumatized mice did not have these symptoms. The Emory team has also determined that an OPRL1 gene variation is more common in people with PTSD.

Other, older studies have suggested that people who are given morphine right after a traumatic event are less likely to develop PTSD. And newer research has suggested (although results are unclear) that administration of the beta blocker propranolol doesn't erase memories in people with PTSD but when taken within six hours of the event, may blunt or dampen the memories' "negative emotional content."

The implications of this vein of research are startling. If "therapeutic forgetting" agents were to be rolled out for wider use, does that mean medics or military personnel themselves should carry doses to administer whenever a traumatic event takes place? What about rape victims? Should they be medicated with a traumatic-memory-dampening drug? If thousands of people in a community experience a violent hurricane, should the drug simply be added to their water supply? And what about victims of and witnesses to genocide? Should the horror they feel—that we all feel—as a result of such atrocities be pre-empted by a prescription?

Ethically the fundamental question is: Do we have the right to erase some or all of our natural responses to bad experiences—before we even think and feel those responses? And if we do have that right, is it really good for us personally or for humanity as a whole?

The main belief that undergirds my life's work is that grief is not only normal but necessary, and that the many thoughts and feelings we experience after a loss—no matter how traumatic—are necessary for us not only to experience but also to express if we are to fully integrate the loss into our continued living. Intervening in that process with a drug designed to trick us into believing we never experienced the loss in the first place (or that it wasn't as bad as it really was) is a recipe for disaster.

Yes, by all means, let's prevent as many traumas as we can. Human beings' proclivity for violence is at the root of a large percentage of PTSD cases, so the more we foster the values of education, transparency, and kindness, the more we will obviate the need for discussions about traumatic grief. Advances in technology may even subdue natural disasters one day. But when traumas do happen, for God's sake, let's not pretend they didn't.

PTSD AND THE BIOLOGICAL/SPIRITUAL CHASM

It is truly wonderful that medical science continues to create ever-clearer instruction manuals to the biology of the human body. How far we have come from the days of leeches and "humors"! *Of course* I laud and support developments such as vaccines, germ theory, and DNA. Who wouldn't?

The brain seems to be the last great frontier of medical science, and its study has already led to astonishing improvements in the treatment of diseases like clinical depression, Parkinson's, and paralysis. Some researchers and thinkers believe that one day soon we will be able to yoke the biology of the brain and technology together to do things like record memories and play them in someone else's head and re-upload memories into the brains of people with Alzheimer's. All I can say is *Wow!*

I part ways with the strictly biochemical understanding of PTSD and the technologies that can interact with that biochemistry because of my belief in the soul. Do you think we are nothing more than the composite of our molecules, cells, and synapses? If so, then the medical model of PTSD is for you. If, on the other hand, you believe, as I do, that the consciousness of human beings exists *apart from* our bodies and may pre-exist and continue on in some form after the death of our bodies, then a physical-only model of PTSD assessment and treatment is sorely lacking. The structural correlates and biochemical markers of PTSD are just *part* of the picture.

Do you believe love is a condition that cannot be grasped as a mere biochemical reaction? Do you believe in the intrinsically spiritual nature of life and death? Do you believe that loss creates grief, which is foremost and fundamentally a spiritual journey—not a biochemical disorder—of the heart and soul? If your answer to these three questions is "Maybe" or "Yes," I invite you to read on.

CHAPTER FIVE

Fear, withdrawal, and negativity in normal grief

In Chapter Three, I briefly mentioned that fear, withdrawal, and numbing are common components of normal, uncomplicated grief as well as PTSD. In order to better compare and contrast these symptoms in normal grief from their presentation in PTSD/traumatic grief, let's take a closer look at the former here.

> "No one ever told me that grief felt so like fear."
>
> — C.S. LEWIS

FEAR IN NORMAL GRIEF

The body's fight-or-flight response, which we reviewed in depth in the last chapter, is also activated with loss of any kind. Consider how you feel when, say, you are out shopping and realize your wallet is missing.

Your heart rate increases, pushing blood to your muscles, heart, and other vital organs.

Your breathing rate increases so you can take in more oxygen.

Your pupils dilate so you can see better.

Your brain receives the extra oxygen and goes into hyper-alert status.

In other words, your body tenses for action, and so you feel a sudden jolt of fear. The same thing happens when you first learn of significant losses in your life, like the loss of a job, a request for separation or divorce from a partner, and, of course, the death of a loved one.

In cases in which the fear response isn't merely a temporary warning—"Oh, no! Where's my wallet? Oh! Now I remember! I put it in my jacket pocket. Here it is!"—phase two of the fight-or-flight response also kicks in. The HPA axis is activated, leading to the release of the stress hormone cortisol to *keep* you in hyper-alert mode.

As with PTSD, however, this lingering fight-or-flight response in the face of profound loss can be a challenge. After all, we cannot run away from our losses. And we typically can't fight them either. While our fear response might help us find our wallet, try to get our job back (or find another job), and search for ways to put our marriage back on track, it cannot magically reverse most losses. Whether we fight the change or not, jobs sometimes disappear. Marriages dissolve. And people we love die.

So when we are grieving, we are often left with this feeling of fear, which transforms over time into worry and anxiety.

In grief, anxiety is typically generated from thoughts such as: "Will my life have any purpose after this loss? Will I ever be happy again? I don't think I can live like this." We also worry that in the wake of one loss, we are vulnerable to more losses. "What if my wife loses her job, too? What if my children won't want to spend time with me after the divorce? What if other people I love die?" Significant loss naturally threatens our feelings of security and stability, and so it is normal to worry and feel anxious.

When we lose something or someone we value, it's also common for us to feel like we're "going crazy," which in turn compounds our fear. Because normal thoughts and behaviors in grief are so different from what one normally experiences, the grieving person does not know whether her new thoughts and behaviors are normal or abnormal.

Often present is a sense of restlessness, agitation, impatience, and ongoing confusion. An analogy that seems to fit is that it is like being in the middle of a wild, rushing river, where you can't get a grasp on anything. Disconnected thoughts race through the griever's mind, and strong emotions at times are overwhelming. Disorganization and confusion often express themselves as an inability to complete any task. A project may get started but go unfinished. Time is distorted and seen as something to be endured. Often, early morning and late at night are moments when the griever feels most disoriented and confused.

Disorganization and confusion are often accompanied by fatigue and lack of initiative, what I often call "the lethargy of grief." The acute pain of the loss is devastating to the point that normal pleasures do not seem to matter. Anhedonia and listlessness set in.

If the loss was the death of a loved one, a restless searching for the person who died is a common part of the experience. Yearning for the dead person and being preoccupied with memories of him may lead to intense moments of distress. Often a shift in perception makes the griever think that other people look like the dead person. A phenomenon sometimes exists whereby sounds are interpreted as signals that the person has returned, such as hearing the garage door open and the person entering the house as she had done for so many years. In fact, visual hallucinations occur so frequently in normal grief that they cannot be considered abnormal. I personally prefer the term "memory picture" to visual hallucination. Seemingly, as part of the searching and yearning process, the griever not only experiences a sense of the dead person's presence but may have transient experiences of looking across the room and seeing the person.

Dreams about the loss are also often a part of the normal grief experience. In the case of the death of someone loved, dreams are often an unconscious means of searching for the person who died. These dreams are often described to me by people as an opportunity to be close to the person. As one widower related, "I don't seem to have any control over it, but each night I find myself dreaming about my wife. I see us together, happy and content. If it only could be that way again." For other people, the dreams are not happy but rather nightmares in which they re-experience the loss or strive to overturn the loss, only to be thwarted.

And so, ongoing fear, worry, and anxiety can be as much a part of normal grief as they are a part of PTSD. Disorganization, confusion, flashbacks, hallucinations/ memory pictures, and nightmares are not uncommonly part of normal grief's fear response.

AVOIDANCE AND EMOTIONAL/SPIRITUAL WITHDRAWAL IN NORMAL GRIEF

Another of the hallmark symptoms of PTSD is avoidance. People who avoid thoughts, feelings, or conversations about the traumatic event or activities, places, or other people that remind them of the event are considered to be exhibiting avoidance. Sometimes, rarely, this avoidance manifests as psychogenic amnesia.

In normal grief, avoidance of people and places associated with the loss is also not uncommon. If you are fired from a job, one typical response is to intentionally avoid the vicinity of that workplace and the haunting grounds of those former coworkers. If someone you love dies, you may avoid her belongings, her bedroom, her photos, and any reminder of her, at least for a while. Sometimes the avoidance of normal grief is halfhearted—"I'd rather not go into Sara's room to get that book I need, but I will..."—and sometimes, in extreme cases, as in PTSD, it seems crippling—"I'm not leaving the house because I can't bear running into people who knew Sara."

Regardless of its amplitude, avoidance in normal grief can be seen as a component of the typical and necessary emotional/spiritual withdrawal. I believe that the natural depression of grief plays an essential role. After we have sustained the profound injury of a significant loss, depression forces us to regroup—physically, cognitively, emotionally, socially, and spiritually. When we are depressed, we instinctively turn inward. We withdraw. We slow down. It's as if our soul presses the pause button and says, "Whoa, whoa, whoaaa. Time out. I need to acknowledge and ruminate on what's happened here before I can consider what I want to do next."

I sometimes call the necessary withdrawal of grief "sitting in your wound." When you sit in the wound of your grief, you surrender to it. You acquiesce to the instinct to slow down and turn inward. You allow yourself to appropriately be troubled by the pain of your loss. You shut the world out for a time so that, eventually, you have created space to let the world back in.

While grief affects all aspects of a griever's life—her physical, cognitive, emotional, social, and spiritual selves—it is fundamentally a spiritual journey. In grief, your understanding of who you are, why you are here, and whether or not life is worth living is challenged. A significant loss plunges you into what C.S. Lewis, Eckhart Tolle, and various Christian mystics have called "the dark night of the soul."

Often, life suddenly seems meaningless. Nothing makes sense. Everything you believed and held dear has been turned upside-down. The structure of your world collapses. Think back to the significant losses in your own life. Did you feel to any degree this sense of emptiness and despair?

The dark night of the soul can be a long and very black night indeed. People struggling with depression and withdrawal after a loss are inhabiting that long, dark night. It is uncomfortable and scary. The pain of that place can seem intolerable, and yet the only way to emerge into the light of a new morning is to experience the night. As a wise person once observed, "Darkness is the chair upon which light sits."

The fifteenth-century monk Thomas à Kempis was an even earlier thought leader on this subject. "Levity of heart and neglect of our hearts," he wrote, "make us insensible to the proper sorrows of the soul. Is there anyone who enjoys everything as he wishes? Neither you, nor I, nor anyone else on earth. There is no one in the world without trouble or anxiety, be he King or Pope." What Lewis and Eckhart recognized, and Kempis before them, is that there are indeed proper sorrows of the soul. In other words, things happen in life that do and should make us sad and anxious. And so, properly, we grieve.

When we are in grief, we naturally withdraw, and our withdrawal allows for the transition from "soul work" to "spirit work." According to the groundbreaking thinking of Carl Jung, "soul work" is the downward movement of the psyche. It is the willingness to connect with what is dark, deep, and not necessarily pleasant. "Spirit work," on the other hand, involves the upward, ascending movement of the psyche. It is during spirit work that grievers find renewed meaning and joy in life.

Soul work comes before spirit work. Soul work lays the foundation for spirit work. The spirit cannot ascend until the soul first descends. The withdrawal, slowing down, and stillness of loss create the conditions necessary for soul work.

NEGATIVE COGNITION AND MOOD IN NORMAL GRIEF

In PTSD, the DSM-5 criterion of negative cognition and mood may manifest as two or more of the following: an inability to remember significant aspects of the event; persistent and exaggerated negative beliefs about oneself, others, and the world; persistent, distorted thoughts about the cause or consequences of the event; persistent negativity; markedly diminished interest or participation in significant activities; feelings of detachment or estrangement from others; and/or a persistent inability to experience positive emotions. Many of these symptoms are also common in normal grief.

When you are grieving a significant loss, it is normal to experience a decreased interest in activities that you have always enjoyed, for example. In the throes of an unexpected, unwanted divorce, is the spurned spouse happy? Does he continue to play golf, cook elaborate meals, and initiate social activities with his buddies (or whatever his normal significant activities are)? Probably not.

Estrangement from others in normal grief often looks like the withdrawal I discussed in the last several pages. During times of profound grief, relationships may naturally suffer because the griever often self-isolates and appropriately focuses on his own inner turmoil. The emotional/spiritual nature of grief makes it, to some degree at least, a solo, internal activity. While our job as caregivers is to urge expression and sharing of this internal struggle, we must ultimately respect the fact that grief is, at bottom, an individual's coming to terms with the reality and unavoidability of loss in life.

And how does loss stereotypically make us feel? Sad. While as I've said, grief may and usually does include a myriad of feelings, we commonly consider sadness the hallmark symptom of grief. I would posit that the sadness of normal grief and the negativity of PTSD can be similar. People in grief often blame themselves, others, and the world at large for their losses. They feel shame. They feel regret. They feel despair. They see the cup as half full—or even completely broken. They can be negatively Eeyore-like in their appraisal of anything put to them. They are often, at least for a time, profoundly unhappy.

I have also said that general anhedonia—the state of being without pleasure—is extremely common in normal grief. In fact, the flatness of depression, which could be described as a persistent inability to experience positive emotions, is a characteristic symptom of grief. People in grief may appear sad, yes, or anxious, angry, guilty, etc., but it's also not atypical for them to appear…nothing. Observers may note that they seem dulled and lifeless. Beaten down. Blah.

I believe that our souls harbor our "divine spark"—what Meister Eckhart described as "that which gives depth and purpose to our living." When we grieve, our divine sparks sputter like candles in the wind. Many hundreds of people in grief have said to me variations on, "I feel so hopeless" or "I am not sure I can go on living." They are not always sobbing in sorrow but rather baldly and flatly stating a fact. The losses that have touched their lives have naturally muted, if not extinguished, their divine sparks. They no longer feel the warm glow of their divine spark inside them. Instead, everything feels dark, cold, and most of all, empty.

Before we move on, I would also like to take this opportunity to point out our cultural bias about so-called negative emotions. The emotions of grief (and PTSD) are often referred to as being "negative," as if they are inherently bad emotions to experience. This judgment feeds our culture's attitude that these emotions should be denied or "overcome." In reality, dark emotions are care-eliciting symptoms that indicate the need for comfort and support. Emotions are not bad or good. They just are. And if we're paying attention, they're there to teach us something.

CHAPTER SIX

Traumatic grief as a form of complicated grief

Grief is the sum total of all the thoughts and feelings you experience when you lose something or someone of great value to you. Grief is normal, natural, and necessary after a loss. In coming chapters I will talk more about mourning, which is the equally essential outward expression of grief.

> "Often it isn't the initiating trauma that creates seemingly insurmountable pain, but the lack of support after."
>
> — S. KELLEY HARRELL

Some grief caregivers refer to the process of open, active, and communicative grief and mourning as "good" grief. Good grief and active mourning create conditions for the healthy integration of loss and foster good mental health. Good grief, however, can turn bad. If normal grief strays off course, it can go on and on without the grieving person ever reaching reconciliation.

I'd also like to point out here that sometimes grief is complicated, and sometimes mourning is complicated. Though I'm using the terms "complicated grief" and "traumatic grief" in this book, the truth is that the symptoms and presentation dictate whether someone is experiencing complicated grief or complicated mourning. Essentially, the person who is primarily internalizing symptoms (such as the person who is depressed or panicked inside but is attempting to hide or deny these feelings) may be said to be experiencing complicated grief, while the person who is expressing dramatic or recalcitrant symptoms (such as the person who makes his anger known through aggressive behavior) may be said to be experiencing complicated mourning. Often what's happening is a mixture of both—a kind of complicated grief and mourning soup.

Having said that, I would like to share ten factors I have observed over the years that often contribute to complicated grief:

TEN FACTORS THAT CAN CONTRIBUTE TO COMPLICATED GRIEF

1. The specific circumstances of the loss
2. The griever's personality, including the ability to understand and access emotionality
3. In the case of the death of someone loved, the griever's relationship with the person who died
4. The griever's access to and use of support systems
5. The griever's cultural/ethnic background
6. The griever's religious/spiritual/philosophical background and current worldview
7. The griever's concurrent stressors
8. The griever's family systems influences
9. The griever's participation in meaningful ceremonies
10. Losses that tend to be stigmatized

1. The specific circumstances of the loss

A traumatic event is a dramatic example of loss circumstances that can complicate grief. The event is typically but not always sudden and/or unexpected. It is also usually violent. We've already discussed what could be considered a "traumatic" loss at some length.

But here I would like you to consider that the traumatic loss event may include circumstances that **even in untraumatic situations could complicate grief**, such as

- out-of-order deaths or injuries (physical or spiritual). Whenever children or younger people are affected, we instinctively feel that the loss is a tragedy and very, very wrong.

- uncertainty surrounding the loss. When it's unclear why an event happened or who may have been at fault, when information about the loss is withheld, or when a traumatic event kills people but their bodies are mutilated and so cannot be viewed by grievers or the bodies are simply irrecoverable/missing, grief is often complicated.
- the griever's sense of culpability. Guilt often complicates grief in circumstances such as car accidents and wartime traumas (soldiers often feel that as "warriors," they should have been able to prevent the death of a fellow service member), but it also arises in more natural loss situations, such as illnesses in which grievers feel they may have made poor medical decisions or divorces in which one or both parties feels unbearably responsible.

2. *The griever's personality, including the ability to understand and access emotionality*

   Self-efficacy comes into play in grief. People who struggle with self-sufficiency in general often struggle with how to navigate in the aftermath of loss. Those who have a demonstrated history of difficulty integrating grief/loss into their lives are more at risk for complicated grief whenever a new loss arises. Also, complicated grief is more common in people who tend to form ambivalent, conflicted, or abusive relationships. These tendencies are often, but not always, a family-of-origin issue.

   Likewise, people who deny or "stuff" emotionality—consciously ("I don't need to cry/get all emotional") or unconsciously—can easily experience complicated grief. Some of these people also have a tendency to intellectualize or to try to "manage" their losses and may seem to be holding it together on the outside, but are often, on the inside, struggling with feelings of emptiness, anger, and other dark emotions.

   In traumatic grief, "loss overload" can hamper both self-efficacy and the ability to access emotionality. After experiencing a traumatic event, people who were formerly self-sufficient and effectively emotional can sometimes, understandably, no longer process their thoughts and feelings. The magnitude of the event, or their internal response to it, is too great for them to thrive using

PTSD: RISK FACTORS AND RESILIENCE

Why do some people develop PTSD after a traumatic event and some do not?

The risk factors for PTSD are essentially a subset of the risk factors for complicated grief: traumatic loss circumstances, a history of mental illness, lack of social support, and concurrent stressors. Nonetheless, people with these risk factors do not necessarily go on to experience PTSD.

People with the magical quality called "resilience" cope better in the face of challenges and loss. They adapt. They bounce back. They are certainly not immune to tragedy. In fact, resilience requires exposure to adversity. It is only after the experience of significant stress that one can be deemed resilient.

Studies show that resilient people are blessed with caring and supportive relationships. The friends and family members of the resilient person provide love and trust, are good role models, and offer encouragement.

Resilient people also have good communication and problem-solving skills, the ability to make plans and carry them out, the capacity to manage strong feelings, and a belief in their own self-efficacy.

When it comes right down to it, I believe that many resilient people are good at mourning (see Chapter Eight). Like all of us, they suffer great and sometimes traumatic losses, and when they do, they instinctively dose themselves with the six central needs of mourning. They acknowledge what has happened, and they feel and express their strong feelings. Trusting that they can emerge from and build on challenges, they incorporate the losses into their self-identities. They turn to others for support. These are the resilient people who fully integrate each loss and go on to live and love without reservation. They should be our role models for traumatic grief reconciliation.

Then there are the seemingly resilient people who are actually carrying their grief (see Chapter Ten). On the outside, these people seem to take loss in stride, but on the inside they are "stuffing" their true feelings instead of feeling them and denying or intellectualizing instead of suffering. They should not be our role models for traumatic grief reconciliation, but are, I fear, the "success stories" of many a medical-model PTSD treatment program.

Authentic mourning builds resilience, and resilience results, at least in part, from authentic mourning. I think we can all agree that most people with PTSD would benefit from resilience-building. The goal of certain therapies (such as cognitive behavioral therapy), in fact, is essentially to grow resilience. But let's not confuse true resilience with grief carrying. When our programs and treatments assuage short-term symptoms but engender perhaps more subtle but also more stultifying long-term consequences, we are robbing Peter to pay Paul.

their former coping skills alone. So, personality and emotional intelligence play a role in complicated grief, and a seeming change in personality and emotional intelligence can be taken as a symptom that the griever is struggling and needs additional support.

3. *In the case of the death of someone loved, the griever's relationship with the person who died*

   While this is only sometimes a factor in traumatic grief, I am including it here because it is often a contributor to complicated grief. People who have unreconciled conflict with or ambivalence for a loved one who dies traumatically commonly run into challenges in their grief. The rockiness often stems from a history of abuse, intermittent break-ups in the relationship, mental health issues, drug or alcohol abuse, and/or codependence emotionally, physically, or financially.

4. *The griever's access to and use of support systems*

   People who are alone in life—no partner (or an uncommunicative partner), no friends, no close colleagues—are at risk for complicated grief because grief demands the ongoing support of others.

   Traumatized grievers, especially, need social support and often need specialized social support. Their grief experience is naturally complicated by the traumatic nature of the loss, and they need the ongoing compassion and understanding of people who have gone through a similar experience and/or are trained to create a safe place for their intense symptoms to be expressed.

   Of course, those whose personalities preclude them from seeking or accepting such support (see number 2) are at risk for complicated grief, as are those whose support systems judge their grief as abnormal or encourage them to "get over it" and "move on."

5. *The griever's cultural/ethnic background*

   Some cultures are better at embracing emotionality and loss than others. When you grow up in a culture that treats grief and loss as "something we don't talk about," you yourself are likely to judge your own feelings of grief as abnormal and wrong.

In general, North Americans tend to be emotion-phobic, which is a drastic mismatch for the traumatized griever. An extreme example is the treatment of Vietnam veterans after the war. Traumatized by their experience, they came home to a culture that not only ignored their normal and necessary grief but blamed them for its genesis.

6. *The griever's religious/spiritual/philosophical background and current worldview*

   As with cultural background, the griever's religious background can complicate grief. Some faiths overtly espouse the message that if you are a strong believer, you do not need to grieve and mourn because a) God does everything for a reason (and you don't need to understand His reasons) and b) this trouble-filled life on Earth is only temporary and is followed by an everlasting life of joy.

   Sometimes traumatized grievers turn to or are sent to prescriptive clergypeople, who in turn tell the griever how to think and behave in the aftermath of the loss. Any "support" grievers receive that does not witness and accept them as they are but rather dictates what is right and wrong can contribute to complicated mourning.

7. *The griever's concurrent stressors*

   The number and magnitude of grievers' concurrent stressors can easily complicate their grief. A history of mental health challenges, such as depression or anxiety, often exacerbates those same symptoms in normal grief and can really magnify them in traumatic grief. Other stressors, such as compromised health and financial challenges, can also complicate grief.

   Traumatic grief often stems from an event that itself created multiple losses, or stressors. Many people might have died or been injured. Homes and belongings may have been destroyed. Add these *on top of* other, more garden-variety stressors in the griever's life (an aging parent, young children who require constant care, normal bills) and you definitely have a recipe for complicated grief.

8. *The griever's family systems influences*

   Children learn how to express or inhibit emotions from their parents and other close family members and usually grow up to be adults who follow suit. Grievers from a "closed" family system are more likely to deny, repress, convert, or avoid the need to mourn. Other family challenges, such as a history of rocky or codependent relationships, can contribute to complicated grief, especially when a traumatic event is involved.

9. *The griever's participation in meaningful rituals*

   Throughout all of history and across all cultures, humans have turned to ritual to mark important life transitions and process thoughts and feelings too profound to handle in everyday conversations and routines. After a death, the funeral helps grievers acknowledge and begin to embrace the painful reality of the loss. It also provides a culturally sanctioned time and place for grievers to support one another. I often say that a meaningful funeral assists with reality, recall, support, expression, meaning, and transcendence.

   In the aftermath of a traumatic event, rituals can also be extremely helpful to grievers. That is why ceremonies long after the event continue to be held at Ground Zero and other trauma sites. In my own practice, I use a minimum of three ceremonies, spread out over time, with anyone I counsel for traumatic grief. From simple candle-lighting rituals (in which the griever lights one candle representing each of his most prominent feelings about the trauma, honoring and embracing each feeling as he talks about it), to writing and burning letters to anyone for whom the griever has unreconciled feelings that relate to the trauma, to creating and ritually using a small shrine in honor of the many losses created by the trauma, such ceremonies accommodate traumatic grief in ways nothing else can.

   Grievers whose loss is not recognized by ritual, on the other hand, or who choose not to or cannot (because of distance, for example) participate in such rituals are at risk for complicated grief because sometimes only ritual is "big" enough to give shape to what happened.

   Of course, for some traumatized grievers, such as rape victims, public ceremony is not appropriate or forthcoming. For these people, creating more intimate, customized rituals in the context of a support group or even individual counseling is a way to tap into the power of ceremony as a therapeutic tool.

10. Losses that tend to be stigmatized

Certain loss circumstances tend to be stigmatized, such as suicide, homicide, death by certain illnesses (such as AIDS), perinatal loss, same-sex loss, and, of course, PTSD. These types of losses are typically not openly acknowledged, publicly mourned, or socially supported. The people who experience such losses naturally grieve inside, but because there is a social stigma surrounding the nature of the loss, they are at greater risk for what is called "disenfranchised grief." Social support is often lacking, and not uncommonly, the griever's sense of culturally instilled shame makes them question the legitimacy of their grief and their right to openly mourn.

Other kinds of losses that may fit in this category are not stigmatized so much as overlooked or minimized, such as the death of an older adult, ex-spouse, or coworker. These circumstances can also create disenfranchised and thus complicated grief.

You might be able to think of other factors that can turn good grief into complicated grief. In the context of PTSD, certainly the traumatic nature of the loss alone is likely to complicate the grief of those it affects. This is why I say that traumatic grief is inherently a form of complicated grief. But when you are working with someone who has PTSD, I urge you to consider the other factors listed above as well. Often the cause of PTSD is not the traumatic event alone but a combination of factors that together have exceeded a person's ability to cope.

HOW COMPLICATED GRIEF PRESENTS

We've reviewed a number of the factors that commonly contribute to complicated grief and/or complicated mourning. But when a person seeking help walks into your office, what does complicated grief look like?

In my work as a grief counselor and educator, I am often faced with the need to untangle the subtle differences among expressions of complicated grief. I only use this framework to assist me in creating a plan of action to be of the most help I possibly can. Below I outline the framework I use at my Center for Loss and Life Transition. Keep in mind these categories are not always neatly defined or mutually exclusive:

Absent or delayed grief

Absent or delayed grief is grief that seems to be nonexistent. When someone experiences a loss but is not given the opportunity (or does not perceive a need) to mourn, grief may seem to be absent but is only, in fact, delayed or "carried." (See page 102.) This happens to some people in their childhood and teenage years if they are "forgotten mourners." Of course, after a significant loss, denial is normal and necessary for a short time, during those early days of shock and numbness, but ongoing denial or postponement is harmful and a sign of complicated grief.

In many situations, PTSD is a form of delayed mourning. For example, in the military, if a service member next to you is killed, you don't lay your gun down in order to mourn. You are actually trained to keep fighting. Months, or sometimes years, later you return home. Now safe, you begin to have symptoms that reflect the need for what I call "catch-up mourning" (see Chapter Eleven). Depending on the nature of your symptoms, you may be labeled with PTSD.

Distorted grief

Distorted grief is grief that seems to focus on one particular thought or feeling. Instead of the symptoms softening, it hardens and gets locked in place—thus it is distorted and covers up underlying emotions like hurt, pain, fear, and helplessness. If someone who has experienced a significant loss is extremely angry all the time, to the exclusion of other grief dimensions, for example, I would suspect complicated grief. I also often see distorted grief expressing itself as depression (where the normal and necessary sadness of grief becomes clinical depression), guilt (where the person self-punishes), or acute anxiety (where symptoms such as panic attacks and hyper-arousal dominate).

Converted grief

Converted grief can have a number of appearances.

One is grief in which the intense feelings of loss are displaced or directed at other situations or people. For example, some grievers with converted grief begin to have trouble at work or in relationships with other people. They may feel depressed, bitter, and hateful, yet unaware that those feelings are, in actuality, tied to their loss.

Other times converted grief is replaced. If the griever takes the emotions that were invested in a relationship that ended in death, for example, and reinvests them prematurely in another relationship, he may be attempting to replace his grief. This replacement pattern does not only occur with other relationships, but in other life activities as well. For example, he may become a workaholic although he has never been one in the past.

Sometimes converters minimize or intellectualize their grief. If they are aware of their feelings of grief but try to downplay them, or if they try to prove to themselves that the loss doesn't affect them very much, they may be minimizing their grief. Or they may talk openly about how "well they are doing" and how "their life is back to normal," even though the loss is recent.

Finally, some converters somaticize their grief by converting their emotions into physical symptoms. Grievers can become so completely preoccupied with their physical problems that they have little or no energy to relate to other people or do their work of mourning.

Other converters exchange their grief for addictive behaviors. Many abuse drugs or alcohol, but others become addicted to exercise, shopping, sex, gambling, or other repetitive physical actions. This is a very common presentation of complicated grief—one that merits the assistance of a skilled and compassionate grief counselor.

Chronic grief

In chronic grief, grievers experience acute symptoms of grief (inability to experience pleasure, confusion, difficulty focusing, lethargy, and others) that do not change or soften over time. Chronic grief tends to be globalized. That

PTSD IN CHILDREN AND TEENS

Of course we wish it were not so, but the reality is that children and teenagers often experience traumatic events. Some experience natural disasters and serious accidents, such as car crashes, while others witness or are personally harmed in school shootings and other violent crimes. Still others are victims of sexual, physical, or psychological abuse. And many suffer the death or serious injury of someone they love as a result of a traumatic event.

In fact, the sheer number of children and teens who experience a traumatic event is rather bracing. As many as 43 percent experience a trauma, and of these, up to 15 percent of girls and six percent of boys go on to develop PTSD.

The symptoms of PTSD in young people can be somewhat different from those of adults. School-aged children seem to be more susceptible to "magical thinking," in which they hold themselves responsible for the trauma or think they could prevent a similar event in the future. They also tend to play out their thoughts and feelings, such as reenacting the event.

Just like adults with PTSD, traumatized child and adolescent grievers have special needs and are particularly deserving of compassionate companionship. They, especially, need our non-clinical empathy and ongoing support. They are not "damaged goods" and should never be made to feel that they are "sick" or have a mental "illness" or disorder. Instead, they are reacting normally to an abnormal or extreme event.

Traumatized children and teens need permission, modeling, and safe places in which to meet their six central needs of mourning. They need parents, guardians, teachers, coaches, bosses, clergy, counselors, and other caring adults in their lives to surround them with compassion and love and to teach them that while life can be extremely painful, it can also be meaningful and joyful. Both ends of the spectrum—and everything in between—need expression and support.

THE PRESCHOOL SUB-TYPE OF PTSD

A new addition to the DSM-5 was the preschool sub-type of PTSD. Traumatized grievers aged six years and younger may exhibit intrusive thoughts, withdrawal, and extreme tempter tantrums. I often say that any child old enough to love is old enough to mourn, so of course young children can and do experience traumatic grief. To heal, they need attentive, around-the-clock care that is sensitive to their changing and often regressive needs and strives to ensure that they feel safe and loved every single moment.

is, no one symptom of grief is dominant, as it is in distorted grief. Rather, the griever continues to actively mourn and seems to place all her energies on the loss. In traumatized grievers, you might see this in people who devote their entire lives to the "cause" of the trauma to the exclusion of other interests, people, and opportunities.

Instead of "complicated grief," the DSM uses the term "Persistent Complex Bereavement Disorder" to describe intense grief that continues to prevent a person from functioning a year or more after a death.

No matter what you call it, complicated grief is grief that has somehow been pulled off the path and needs to find its way back to it. As the PTSD literature so often points out, not everyone who experiences traumatic loss goes on to develop PTSD. According to the National Center for PTSD, about six of every ten American men and five of every ten women will experience at least one trauma in their lives. But while half of us experience a trauma, only seven to eight percent of us will go on to have PTSD.

I would like to suggest that everyone who experiences a trauma suffers some degree of traumatic grief. In other words, grief caused by a trauma *is* traumatic grief. The trauma alone and/or the trauma in combination with some or several of the factors mentioned on pages 54 through 60 may complicate their grief. We could say that traumatic grief is de facto complicated grief, but then so is grief caused by an untimely death, grief in combination with substance abuse, and many other combinations of loss circumstances and individuals' attributes.

To me, what this all boils down to is that the traumatic nature of a loss (and remember, what could be considered "traumatic" from the griever's point of view is itself a gray area; see the chart on page 17) is one of many risk factors for complicated grief. But whether or not the person ends up with a diagnosis of PTSD, traumatic grief, complicated grief, or persistent complex bereavement disorder matters not at all compared to the truly important question of how to help the millions of Americans and hundreds of millions more the world over who are thought to be suffering from PTSD at this very moment.

CHAPTER SEVEN

Medical-model therapies as treatment

Since PTSD was formalized as a diagnosis in the 1980 DSM-III, many studies have been done and books written on the efficacy of various forms of treatment. In this chapter I will very briefly summarize the most widely used treatments and offer my perspective on them through the lens of PTSD as traumatic grief.

> "Communities of like-minded people develop beliefs and practices, teach them to each other, reinforce them as the standard beliefs of the community, and lose sight of the fact that those beliefs and practices are make-do creations."
>
> — ROBERT T. FANCHER

Psychological debriefing

The concept of psychological debriefing in the aftermath of a traumatic event is based on the assumption that when people are given a structured, safe opportunity—not long after the event—to "download" their memories of what happened, as well as their thoughts and feelings about it, and to be assured that their thoughts and feelings are normal, they will be less likely to go on to develop PTSD. Debriefings can be conducted one-on-one, between a therapist and a griever, or in a group setting. Most are designed as single-session debriefings, though sometimes the debriefing might entail two or more meetings.

PTSD research seems to have concluded that psychological debriefings do not, in fact, prevent PTSD. My take on debriefings is that it is impossible to ever completely "release" one's thoughts and feelings about a traumatic loss, let alone in a single meeting. Grief is a long-term journey—especially traumatic grief. And while good supportive care in the early hours and days of post-trauma shock is essential, no immediate therapeutic technique can preempt or "nip in the bud" the traumatic grief that will naturally, and essentially, unfold in the coming months and years.

Early cognitive-behavioral interventions

As you know, cognitive-behavioral therapy (CBT) is a psychotherapeutic approach that teaches the person to use goal-oriented, systematic procedures when "dysfunctional" patterns of thoughts and feelings arise. Early post-trauma CBT has been used as an attempt to educate people in the use of redirecting techniques, so that when they are struggling with common thoughts and feelings in the months after the event, they will have self-correcting skills at their disposal.

Early CBT with ongoing therapeutic monitoring of symptoms can be effective, says the research, though researchers are still trying to pin down methods that will allow them to identify which victims need how much early CBT and monitoring.

To my way of thinking, early CBT is an attempt to force traumatized grievers to quickly rationalize or "think away" a profoundly spiritual injury before they've even had a chance to begin to plumb the depth and breadth of the injury. While I agree that trauma victims need support in the early days and weeks after the event, thinking-skills training is inadequate and, in fact, relying on it alone is detrimental to people's long-term well-being and self-actualization. To me, a central principle of compassionate caregiving is that caregivers must enter into what grievers think and feel without believing that their job is to *change* what the grievers think and feel.

Short-term cognitive behavioral therapy

Many studies have been done on the effectiveness of various CBT techniques on PTSD, including exposure therapy, cognitive processing therapy, stress inoculation training, and others. The course of treatment is typically short, ranging from six to 15 sessions of an hour or two each, once or twice a week. Usually the sessions are individual, but sometimes they are structured as group meetings.

Of the short-term therapies, the most widely studied has been exposure therapy, in which people are guided through re-imagining and describing the traumatic event and are often also physically exposed to low-risk places and activities that remind them of the traumatic experience. Exposure therapy often works, and I believe it is because it doses people with several of their natural needs of mourning (especially Needs 1, 2, 3, and 6; see pages 75 through 87). But still, while exposure therapy is very helpful, it does not necessarily allow the traumatized person to lead with what is, at any given moment, most pressing for her. What if today she is most struggling with the meaning of the event or her despair in trying to find a reason to go on?

Cognitive processing therapy (CPT), which involves helping people become overtly aware of their thoughts, feelings, and changed beliefs since the traumatic event and provides them with tools for "rethinking" those thoughts, feelings, and changed beliefs, has also been proven effective. As with exposure therapy, CPT doses people in several central mourning needs (especially 1, 2, 3, and 5). This is good. But it also runs the risk of essentially communicating to people that their thoughts and feelings are bad or unhealthy and that they simply need to think differently. "Don't think this...think that." That brand of judging and pathologizing does not affirm the normalcy of people's grief.

Stress inoculation training (SIT) also makes the Agency for Health Care Policy and Research's "A list" for treatment of PTSD. In SIT, people are educated about healthy and unhealthy stress responses and taught new skills in emotion regulation, cognitive appraisal, problem-solving, communication, and socialization. During SIT sessions, people ostensibly talk about some of their trauma-related thoughts, feelings, and behaviors, but the focus is on helping replace them with new thoughts, feelings, and behaviors—ones that will help them "cope better." As with CPT, I fear that SIT, in essence, teaches people that their existing thoughts, feelings, and behaviors are "bad" and makes the therapist, rather than the griever, the expert of the grief experience.

Exposure therapy, CPT, SIT, and other forms of CBT likely deserve a place in your PTSD caregiving toolkit, especially if you are already trained in and comfortable with their use. I would ask, however, that you consider superimposing the companioning philosophy of grief care (see Chapter Nine) *on top of* these techniques. How would this new way of looking at traumatic grief and your role in it alter, however subtly, your administration of these therapies? Perhaps the prescriptive language you use would soften. Maybe you would allow more room in the sequencing for newly arisen client needs to take center stage. I also don't believe that any one of these techniques alone provides sufficient care. People with PTSD need and deserve more holistic, soul-based care.

EVIDENCE-BASED PSYCHOTHERAPY AND GRIEF

In medicine today, evidence-based treatment hangs the moon. For the most part, this makes sense. If a certain surgical approach results in better range of motion for people, or if a particular drug cocktail creates longer remission, then by all means, let's all get on the same page and follow those best practices.

In mental health, evidence-based therapy is also all the rage. While I understand the desire to help people in the best way possible, and I agree that we are learning effective ways to measure and treat some mental health issues, I also believe that grief does not lend itself well to objective measurement and treatment.

First, grief is an exceedingly complex and variable response to loss and is comprised of physical, cognitive, emotional, social, and spiritual symptoms. And second, while in part it makes itself known in the body, it is fundamentally a condition of the soul.

Today, various standardized assessments are used to measure the severity of PTSD, including the PTSD Symptom Scale (there are several types), the PTSD Checklist, the PTSD Diagnostic Scale, the Impact of Event Scale, the CAPS Scale, and others. These tools try to assign a number to an individual's traumatic grief. This number, then, ends up being the criterion by which any given treatment's "success" is judged.

Companioning people who are struggling with grief is more art than science, more heart than head. While caregivers can employ assessment scales at the beginning and end of therapy to reveal numerical "progress," in reality results can only be subjectively measured. How do you measure a person's newfound ability to be more in touch with and expressive of her feelings, even when those feelings are painful? How do you measure a person's renewed capacity for hope and joy?

Has your life ever been changed profoundly for the better because of your relationship with a certain teacher, friend, or partner? If so, you understand something of the art of human interaction and well-being. Even in this era of evidence-based everything, the soul defies measurement. As Albert Einstein astutely observed, "Not everything that counts can be counted."

Drug therapy

In Chapter Three I briefly summarized the body's fight-or-flight response when it is exposed to a dangerous stressor, including the cascade of neurotransmitters and hormones that flood the body. I also discussed the understanding, gleaned from brain imaging, that in PTSD these biochemicals are likely wholly or in part responsible for the refractory, heightened nature of the body's fear response—what people sometimes describe as the "I'm stuck in that terrible moment" quality of PTSD.

While psychopharmacologic agents have not yet been developed specifically to treat PTSD, medications commonly and effectively used to treat depression and other anxiety disorders, especially SSRIs and SNRIs, have been shown to ease PTSD symptoms that interfere with a person's ability to function in his day-to-day life and to participate in therapy.

I support the use of psychopharmacologic agents, when indicated, as one element in a multifaceted approach to helping people suffering from PTSD. For one, fear-based symptoms that are so severe they prevent people from eating, sleeping, grooming, leaving the house, and other essential tasks must first be addressed before more emotional-spiritual repercussions can be considered. Think back to Maslow's hierarchy of needs (page 16). The imminent needs of our bodies must first be met, followed by our psychological need for a sense of safety.

Similarly, symptoms that preclude people from attending therapy sessions or accepting any support from friends and family members may be eased by medication. While to some degree these symptoms are a normal part of traumatic grief in the short-term, it is also necessary for them to soften, so that deeper, longer-term grief work can begin.

Still, despite studies that seem to confirm the effectiveness of certain medications in the treatment of PTSD, I urge extreme caution in their use. In some circles, for example, prescribing anti-anxiety medication, antidepressants, and antipsychotics to those struggling with PTSD or other mental health issues seems to be a matter of course. But most of these people are not receiving concurrent and ongoing therapy. They are being given drugs as a quick and convenient "solution" to their symptoms. Problem is, their symptoms, I would argue, are not strictly biochemical.

They are also—actually, primarily—spiritual. Exposure to violence and atrocities creates deep psychic injuries that can't be fixed with a pill. First and foremost, traumatic grief requires the compassionate support of our fellow human beings.

EMDR

Eye movement desensitization and reprocessing (EMDR) is a fascinating therapeutic technique that has been around since the 1980s. It posits that traumatic memories can remain stuck as "unprocessed memories," causing PTSD symptoms. Through a structured process of guiding the person to recall traumatic images, or mental pictures, usually together with back-and-forth eye or bodily movements, followed by a conjuring of a positive mental images, the therapist ostensibly helps the person process the negative images and replace them with positive ones.

Studies have resoundingly found EMDR effective in the treatment of PTSD. While there are varying brain-biology-based theories as to why this might be so, it is generally believed that EMDR is a close cousin, or maybe even a twin, to exposure therapy.

Any therapeutic technique that encourages the exploration of traumatic memories in a safe, supportive environment gets my vote. While EMDR alone does not constitute an appropriately holistic treatment plan, it does appear that EMDR can be an effective component.

Psychosocial rehabilitation

Programs and treatment that focus on social and occupational functioning instead of symptoms management fall under the heading of psychosocial rehabilitation. This category includes things like patient education, social skills training, and case management. In essence, the goal is to help the person with PTSD become independent once again by retraining him to live, work, and communicate with others.

I'm sure that some PTSD sufferers, those whose psychic injuries are so severe that they cannot function at all, need and deserve the support that psychosocial rehabilitation offers. But first what they need and deserve is help mourning their grief. Without mourning, they will continue to live with and suffer from profound injuries, even if the psychosocial rehabilitation helps them return to what may look, on the surface, like normal life.

A number of other treatments for PTSD have been used and formally studied, including dialectical behavior therapy, relaxation training, hypnosis, and more. If traumatic grief were a pie, I believe that the medical-model-based therapies can lay claim to slices—some skinny and some wide, but never the whole pie. They also tend to denigrate the traumatic grief experience—the entire pie. In their pathologizing, they teach people who are suffering from awful symptoms that they are among the small percentage of people exposed to trauma who have developed "maladaptive responses" or an "illness" or a "disorder." In other words, the pie is bad.

But the pie's not bad. The pie is normal and necessary. Only the event that created the pie was bad.

CHAPTER EIGHT

Mourning as "treatment"

Grief is the sum total of what we think and feel inside when we experience a loss. Mourning is the outward expression of our grief. And mourning, I firmly believe and have observed time and time again, is the key to healing.

> "Give sorrow words; the grief that does not speak whispers the o'er-fraught heart and bids it break."
>
> — WILLIAM SHAKESPEARE

Mourning is treatment, if you will. PTSD sufferers may also need concurrent medical treatment, such as drug therapy, but because their symptoms are, in essence, caused by loss, there is no getting around the fact that mourning is *the* essential component of their often long and arduous journey back to well-being.

Mourning, as I stated in the Introduction, is the missing piece.

I'd like to point out here that I don't usually use the word "treatment" when it comes to grief. The term implies that grief is a disease that must be cured. But as I have emphasized, grief is definitely not a disease. It is the normal and necessary response to an injury caused by significant loss.

But because PTSD or traumatic grief presents as and is thought of as a medical condition by many, **I am using the word treatment here to emphasize that no matter which combination of therapeutic approaches might be prescribed, mourning is essential.** Mourning is always the right thing to facilitate for someone who is grieving.

As I see it, the problem with the current medical-model approach to PTSD care is that it does not fully honor grief and mourning. Rather than allowing for the creation of safe places, or sanctuaries, where hurting people can mourn in doses when their heads and hearts are ready, many of the forms of treatment used in the current model encourage people to hurry up and "recover from" their psychic injuries. Pain and feelings of loss are seen as something to prevent or get beyond as soon as possible. Yet, only if we befriend and experience our wounds do we ultimately "reconcile," not resolve, significant losses.

The medical model of PTSD care has placed the focus on selective symptom relief. While I appreciate the need to first help people with PTSD find relief from their dramatic fear-based symptoms, which are often preventing them from functioning in their daily lives, these symptoms are only the tip of the iceberg that is their life-altering traumatic grief injury.

Traumatic loss changes people's lives forever. And the movement from "before" to "after" is a naturally long, painful journey. From my own experiences with both traumatic and normal grief as well as those of the thousands of grieving people I have companioned over the years, I have learned that if we are to integrate loss into our lives, we cannot skirt the outside edges of our grief. Instead, we must journey all through it, sometimes meandering the side roads, sometimes plowing directly into its raw center.

Mourning is the active part of the journey. Mourning allows wounds to heal. If we don't acknowledge PTSD for what it really is—a grief response following a traumatic event—we actually end up building walls around the unhealed wound in an effort to protect it. Grief is the essence of PTSD. If we continue to avoid acknowledging this truth, the very people we intend to help will often end up continuing to carry around their unhealed wounds. In many ways, mourning is a series of spiritual awakenings borne of the willingness to have an authentic encounter with the pain surrounding the loss. **We can try to "treat" the symptoms, or we can try to help the person discover the courage to surrender to the pain.**

When we as humans experience trauma, we need to actively mourn in order to integrate the many losses caused by the traumatic event into our lives. This is difficult to do when feelings of grief are perceived as weakness in our "buck-up" culture. **Something happens to grief when a culture is drawn to science and leaves art behind. Traumatic grief then becomes something to be resolved and overcome rather than experienced.**

But to be experienced and expressed is what it needs. To facilitate its expression—or mourning—a helpful concept for both grievers and caregivers is that of the six central needs of mourning. The griever's awareness of these needs can help build a participative, action-oriented perception of grief instead of something passively experienced or to be "treated away." Those of you familiar with the literature on grief will note some similarity between what I am calling "the six central needs of mourning" and the observations of others (Worden, Rando, Lindemann, Parkes, and Weiss).

EXPERIENCE

To "experience" literally means to feel or undergo something. One's entire being (physical, cognitive, emotional, social, and spiritual) is involved. "My experience is what I agree to attend to," observed William James. As caregivers, we have an obligation not to resolve or take away symptoms but rather to help our fellow human beings attend to their myriad thoughts and feelings as well as the events that precipitated them.

MOURNING NEED 1: Acknowledge the reality of the losses

This need of mourning involves confronting the reality that the traumatic event happened and that it created in the griever a number of primary and secondary injuries. I have found that acknowledging the full reality of the losses may occur over weeks, months, and sometimes even years. As humans, we can know something in our heads (the cognitive reality) but not in our hearts (the affective reality).

Especially in cases of traumatic grief, the griever may try to push away the reality of the loss at times. It is a sign of healthy discernment to want to protest the reality of the horrific event and the devastation it created. Some degree of denial, especially in the early, shock-filled days following the event, is a healthy coping mechanism.

PRIMARY AND SECONDARY LOSSES IN TRAUMATIC GRIEF

All significant loss is multidimensional. When someone I love dies, I lose much more than the physical presence of that person (the primary loss). Depending on the roles that person played in my life, I may also feel that I have lost my history (a parent), my financial security (a provider partner), and/or my sense of immortality (any death).

The grief set in motion by a traumatic event may or may not cause what we think of as a primary loss for the griever. Back to the example of the tornado. If parts of my town are torn apart by a tornado, I may not lose my life or my house/belongings. I may not even experience the death of someone I know personally or places I own or that were even particularly special to me, but I will still be subject to a number of secondary or fall-out losses. In other words, even if the tornado didn't touch me, my loved ones, or my house, I am still likely to experience some degree of traumatic grief because of the secondary losses.

What follows is a partial list of common secondary losses for grievers in the wake of a traumatic event:

LOSS OF SENSE OF SECURITY

- Physical security: Because of the body's fight-or-flight response, traumatized grievers commonly feel physically unsafe.
- Emotional security: In formerly stable individuals, emotions may now feel out-of-control. Friends and family who had always provided emotional support may now step away.
- Fiscal security: PTSD sufferers whose symptoms prevent them from working may have significant financial concerns. Natural disasters can wreak havoc with finances.

LOSS OF SELF

- Self: "I feel like part of me got left behind at the traumatic event."
- Identity: PTSD sufferers may have to rethink their roles as employees, husbands or wives, mothers or fathers, sons or daughters, best friends, etc.
- Self-confidence: PTSD victims commonly experience negative self-esteem.
- Health: The physical symptoms of fight-or-flight as well as normal grief often create a feeling of physical unwellness.
- Personality: "I just don't feel like myself…"

LOSS OF MEANING

- Goals and dreams: Hopes and dreams for the future can be shattered.
- Faith: Grievers often question their faith.
- Will/desire to live: Traumatized grievers question their futures. They may ask, "Why go on…?"
- Joy: Life's most precious emotion, happiness, is naturally compromised after a traumatic event.

Over time, however, the traumatized griever must slowly, gently, and with the support of others, allow the reality into her head and heart. The griever will often move back and forth between protesting and encountering the reality of the event and the losses that cascaded from it. She will often discover the need to replay the event and confront memories, both good and bad. This replay is a vital part of this need of mourning. It is as if each time the griever talks it out (converts grief into mourning), the traumatic event and the losses it created are a little more real.

We as humans come equipped with an organic capacity to slowly integrate loss into our lives. We can embrace grief and allow it to unfold into mourning. The reality that we as humans are capable of mourning tells us we are meant to gently acknowledge losses and integrate them into our lives. However, we cannot do this alone; we need the support of compassionate friends, family members, and caregivers.

MOURNING NEED 2: Feel the pain of the losses

To be "bereaved" literally means "to be torn apart." When a person is torn apart by traumatic loss, mourning requires embracing the pain of the loss. Symptoms of pain and suffering are usually felt in five domains—physical, cognitive, emotional, social, and spiritual. We've already reviewed common symptoms of normal grief, but here let's look at how the symptoms often "show up" for the traumatized griever in each of these domains:

Physical: Grief naturally results in physical discomfort; the body responds to the stress of the encounter.

Cognitive: Grief naturally results in cognitive discomfort; thought processes are confused and memory is impaired.

Emotional: Grief naturally results in emotional discomfort, and a multitude of wave-like emotions may be experienced that demand comfort and care.

Social: Grief naturally results in social discomfort; the griever may withdraw, and/or friends and family may withdraw, and isolation may result.

Spiritual: Grief naturally results in spiritual discomfort; questions may arise such as, "Why go on living?"; "Will my life have meaning?"; "Where is God in this?"

For many people in our emotion-phobic, mourning-avoidant culture, it is easier to avoid, repress, or deny the pain of grief than it is to confront it. Yet, it is in confronting one's pain and realizing it doesn't mean something is wrong or "pathological" that we ultimately integrate loss into our lives. To heal we must go to the wilderness of our souls.

The opposite of embracing pain is often demonstrated by attempts to stay "in control." In fact, one way that people describe the sensation of PTSD is that they are "out of control." Underlying that controlling impulse is anxiety and fear—the lingering fear caused by the fight-or-flight response as well as the existential fear that the traumatized griever will have to experience even more pain in any or all of the five domains noted above.

When grievers accept that they cannot go around the pain of loss, they often discover the courage to relax into the pain, and therein lies the paradox. Trying to avoid, repress, or deny the pain of grief makes the griever an opponent of the journey and creates more chronic states of anxiety and depression (see carried grief, page 102).

Control appears to be one of North Americans' favorite ways of running from grief and loss. We are so high on control that it has become an internalized illusion that we think we can let go of control by simply wanting to. In other words, we think we can control relinquishing control! Human beings in grief do not let go of control; human beings in grief let go of the belief that we have control.

Spiritual maturity in grief is attained when the griever embraces a paradox—to live in the state of both encounter and surrender while simultaneously "working at" and "surrendering to" the journey As the griever comes to know this paradox, he can very slowly, with no rewards for speed, discover the soothing of his soul. Many grievers have taught me that they actually find themselves wrapped in a gentle peace—the peace of living at once in the encounter (the "grief work") and the surrender (embracing the mystery of not understanding).

In many Eastern cultures, aging, illness, death, and grief are understood differently. When people live in daily contact with these realities, they tend not to deny that life involves pain and suffering. As Western culture has gained the capacity to limit pain and suffering, we tend to encourage the denial of pain.

Advances in medicine and ever-increasing technology to lengthen lifespans have, without doubt, improved the levels of physical comfort for many North Americans. However—this is when a shift in perception seems to have taken place—as pain and suffering have become less visible or have been relegated to behind closed doors, they are no longer perceived as an intrinsic part of the nature of being human, but instead seen as a sign that something has gone wrong.

Through no fault of their own, many grievers, including traumatized grievers, misunderstand the role of pain and suffering. If they openly express their feelings of grief, misinformed friends and family members often advise them to "keep their chin up" or "let go." If, on the other hand, they remain "strong" and "in control," they may well be congratulated for "doing well" with their grief.

Many friends and family members (and sometimes even caregivers) want grieving people to stay in control as a form of self-protection. All of us attempt to control because we are *afraid* of the pain of grief. It hurts to embrace the depths of the loss. It hurts to acknowledge that life is often dangerous, mean, and capricious and to be humbled by our life losses.

Of course, as a caregiver to people in grief, you must become acquainted not only with the pain of others, but also your own pain. If you don't, you will unconsciously want to "fix" people in pain and not create hospitality for them to "dose" themselves with this need.

Yes, an essential part of your helping role is to help the griever dose the pain of the loss. In other words, the griever cannot (nor should she try to) overload herself with the hurt all at one time. In fact, sometimes your role may be to distract the griever from the pain of the loss, while at other times you will need to create a "safe place" for the griever to move toward the pain. Dose the pain: yes! Deny the pain: no!

MOURNING NEED 3: Remember the loss

In normal grief caused by death, grievers have a need to pursue a relationship of memory with the person who died. As Kierkegaard noted, "While life must be lived forward, it can only be understood backwards." Instead of simply ending or forgetting about the relationship, which some medical-based grief models essentially advocate, what grievers actually need to do is convert the relationship from one of presence to one of memory. The love and attachment remain, but the focus of that love and attachment shift. (Grievers who believe that life continues after death, on the other hand, often shift their relationship from one of presence on Earth to one of presence separated, for the time being, by time and space.)

In traumatic grief, the need to remember is a controversial topic. Must traumatized grievers relive the events of the trauma in order to process and integrate the memories? Many, but not all, of the medical-model therapies for treatment of PTSD discussed in Chapter Seven include an element of remembering. Exposure therapy, for example, as well as EMDR, focus on remembering and memory cues, and both have been found effective. Indeed, treatments that include some element of exposure therapy have proven the most powerful and reliable forms of treatment. Techniques to conjure memories include, alone or in combination, imagining (silently, aloud, or in writing); *in vivo* exposure to places and situations that mimic the trauma; and technology-assisted (such as virtual reality). On the other hand, some techniques, such as CBT, may sometimes avoid memory-gathering and sharing altogether.

One issue with remembering the traumatic event that caused so many losses is that people with PTSD often seem to have gaps in their memories—those "hard drive" glitches we talked about earlier. The dissociative quality of the memory also seems to make the event hard, if not impossible, to remember. One interesting study showed that when we experience an event in virtual reality from our own point-of-view, we remember it well. But when we experience the event as an outside observer, we don't remember it well.

Intrusive memories, of course, are also characteristic of PTSD. These are painful, often violent flashes of memory that arise unbidden and shanghai the person's brain, usually when he doesn't want them to. We might say these memories are part of the glitchy technology. But we might also say that they are memories asking to be expressed.

And finally, the PTSD research can't yet say definitively that memory processing is *essential* to healing. While treatments that include memory processing have resoundingly been found effective, others that haven't included memory processing, such as stress inoculation therapy, have also seemed helpful to some people.

So let's summarize what we know about remembering the loss and PTSD. Remembering the event as a component of treatment has been found effective. Sometimes with PTSD it may be impossible to remember some or all of the traumatic event itself. On the other hand, intrusive memories are also common. And finally, it's possible that memory processing as a means of treating PTSD isn't absolutely necessary.

I've said that it's understandable to want to avoid both the reality and the pain of a loss but that acknowledging the loss and embracing the pain are essential to healing. It's also understandable for traumatized grievers to want to avoid their traumatic memories. And why not avoid them? We are all living in a culture that teaches us to move away from instead of toward our grief.

Yet, as with Mourning Needs 1 and 2, I believe that Mourning Need 3 is not optional.

Intentionally circumventing traumatic memories invites carried grief. It's like leaving a significant portion of a wound uncleansed and uncared for, on purpose. While all grief care must be individualized, and the unique needs and circumstances of any particular griever take precedence over generalizations, my understanding of PTSD as traumatic grief suggests that caregivers should create safe conditions for, develop the camaraderie for, and encourage the appropriate sharing of traumatic memories.

To ignore painful or ambivalent memories is to prevent healing from taking place. In the safety of your nonjudgmental, empathetic relationship and with the right timing and pacing, the traumatized griever should be invited to share her memories with you. Memories and grief must have a heart to hold them. In fact, remembering the past makes hoping for the future possible.

You have the honor of being present to the traumatized griever as she discovers that the essence of finding meaning in the future is not to forget the past, but to embrace the past.

MOURNING NEED 4:
Develop a new self-identity

This need of mourning relates to the necessary evolution of a new self-identity based on life as it is now, after the traumatic event, versus life as it was then, before the traumatic event. All of us are forever changed by significant loss. If I am diagnosed with cancer, for example, my self-concept shifts. I used to be healthy. Now I am unhealthy. I used to be invincible. Now I am vulnerable. I used to be a provider for my family. Now I may not be able to provide. At first these forced-upon-me changes in self-identity are painful. They are injuries. They feel like diminishments. Over time, as I integrate them into my being, I may find new opportunities for growth and joy sparkling in the rubble.

Traumatic loss, too, forces changes in self-identity. After a roadside bomb detonates, the platoon leader who had always thought of himself as the protector of his unit must now come to terms with the reality that service members under his command are dead. The woman who was raped must reconstruct her sexuality.

COMPLEMENTARY THERAPIES FOR TRAUMATIC GRIEF

I advocate a holistic approach to caring for traumatized grievers. Any therapy that helps them with the six central needs of mourning and takes into account the knowledge that their grief affects them physically, cognitively, emotionally, socially, and spiritually may be an appropriate part of their care.

Many so-called "complementary" therapies fit the bill. My ironic quote marks stem from the fact that the medical model sees other forms of care as complementary—non-essential add-ons to their foundational and essential care—when in fact complementary therapies may be just as if not more essential to helping traumatized grievers than, say, drug therapy.

Yoga and reiki, for example, might help traumatized grievers with not only the physical symptoms of their grief but also their spiritual journeys. Music therapy can assist with the accessing and expression of deep emotions. Hypnosis may be an avenue to unlocking authentic thoughts and feelings.

As you learn more about the companioning model of grief care in the next chapter, keep in mind that complementary therapies can and should be considered as elements of care for all traumatized grievers.

The mother of a teen who completed suicide must re-conceive what it means to be a mother. The ways all three of them define themselves and the ways in which others define them have changed.

Redefinition of the self in the aftermath of a traumatic loss is a slow process, not a single event in time. Grievers often feel childlike as they struggle with their changing identities. They may exhibit a temporarily heightened dependence on others and experience feelings of helplessness, frustration, inadequacy, and fear. These feelings can be overwhelming and frightening, yet they are a natural response to this important need of mourning.

MOURNING NEED 5: Search for meaning

This need relates to renewing one's rationale for life and living after it has been torn apart. After a significant loss, grievers naturally question the meaning and purpose of life. They review their philosophy of life and explore religious and spiritual values as they work on this need.

"Why" and "How" questions are common when grievers search for meaning. "Why did this happen now, in this way?" "How will I go on living?" The "Why" questions often precede the "How" questions in this unfolding process. This search for a reason to go on living is a vital part of grief work and requires an expenditure of physical, emotional, and spiritual energy.

There is for many traumatized grievers a profound lack of sense of direction or future purpose, particularly if the griever's hopes, dreams, and plans for the future were invested heavily in people, places, or things that were damaged or destroyed in the traumatic event. At times, overwhelming sadness and loneliness may be his constant companions. After all, he is faced with finding some meaning in going on with life even though he feels empty and alone.

Traumatic loss forces grievers to explore their worldviews—that set of beliefs they have about how the universe functions and what place they, as individuals, occupy therein. Some studies have observed that many people in modern Western culture tend to travel through life believing that the world is essentially a nice place in which to live, that life is mostly fair, and that they are basically good people who deserve to have good things happen to them. But when a traumatic event happens, the pain and suffering that result undermine these beliefs and can make it very difficult to continue living this happy life. The result is that through the search for meaning, pain and suffering are intensified.

So, where do traumatized grievers begin their search for meaning and renewal of resources for life and living? For many, the search begins with their religious or spiritual traditions. Doubt often arises. For example, in the Judeo-Christian tradition, a foundational belief is that the universe was created by a good and just God. Traumatic events naturally challenge many grievers' belief in the goodness of God and their understanding that the world is essentially a nice place in which to live.

When such beliefs or longstanding worldviews are challenged in early grief, there is often little, if anything, to replace them right away. This is a part of the "suspension" or "void" that grief initiates—an absence of belief that precedes any renewal of belief. This absence creates liminal space. *Limina* is the Latin word for threshold, the space betwixt and between. When grievers are in liminal space, they are not busily and unthinkingly going about their daily lives. Neither are they living from a place of assuredness about their relationships and beliefs. Instead, they are unsettled. Both their mindless daily routines and their core beliefs have been shaken, forcing them to reconsider who they are, why they're here, and what life means. It's frightening and unpleasant being in liminal space, but that's where traumatic loss takes them. Without loss (which they didn't ask for, by the way), they wouldn't go there. But here's the thing: it is only in liminal space that they can reconstruct their shattered worldviews and re-emerge as transformed, whole people who are ready to live fully again.

Bringing one's torn-apart world back together takes time, loving companions, and humility—that virtue that helps us humans when we face powerlessness. A vital part of helping people search for meaning is encouraging them to mourn without any pressure to provide answers to profound "meaning of life" questions.

Creating sacred space where grievers can hurt and eventually find meaning in continued living are not mutually exclusive. Actually, the need to openly mourn and the need to slowly discover renewed meaning in continued living can and do naturally blend into each other, with the former giving way to the latter as healing unfolds. Our universal calling as human beings is to be the most loving people we can possibly be. In sharing your gift of helping grievers search for meaning after a traumatic event, you may well have found your calling.

MOURNING NEED 6:
Receive ongoing support from others

This need acknowledges the reality that traumatized grievers need support long after the traumatic event. Because mourning is a "dosed" process that unfolds over time, support must be available for months and even years after the event. The quality and quantity of support the griever receives is a major influence on the capacity to integrate the loss into her life and renew resources for living.

Unfortunately, because our society places so much emphasis on returning to "normal" within a brief period of time, many grieving people are abandoned shortly after a traumatic event. When possible, an essential ingredient of your companioning role is to support the griever not only in the period of acute grief, but over the long term.

To be truly helpful, the people who make up the support system must appreciate the impact the event and all its fall-out losses have had and are having on the griever. They must understand that in order to slowly reconcile the losses, the griever must be allowed—even encouraged—to mourn long after the traumatic event. And they must perceive grief not as an enemy to be vanquished but as a necessity to be experienced as a result of having established meaningful connections in life.

As you care for the griever, you will learn about the support he may or may not receive from individual family members or friends, from faith communities, or from other groups that are a part of his life. You will learn that some grievers openly seek and accept support, while others are more likely to have difficulty opening themselves to the support that is available to them. Some traumatized grievers will teach you that the stigmatized circumstances of the loss (suicide, homicide, rape) have impacted the offering of support from others. Often, the greater the stigma, the less the support available and the higher the risk for what is called mutual pretense: when people around the griever know what has happened but believe they should not talk about it with the survivor.

A FAMILY-SYSTEMS APPROACH IN PTSD

Traumatic loss ripples across families, neighborhoods, cities, far-flung friend networks, and even generations.

In a family, sometimes all the members are exposed to the traumatic event, as in the case of a natural disaster, and sometimes just one member experiences the traumatic event, as in the case of a military service member or a sexual-assault victim. But regardless of which and how many family members were personally involved in the traumatic event, the entire family is affected.

From a traumatic-grief perspective, it's helpful to think of the entire family as injured. Each individual in the family sustains a psychic injury with its own unique symptoms, and the family as a collective whole also sustains an injury. Then there are the secondary ripples of loss caused by PTSD, when the primary griever's ongoing symptoms continue to affect individuals within the family as well as the family as a whole.

The impact of PTSD on the family is like a pressure cooker: everyone has a need to feel understood but, wounded as they are, little capacity to be understanding. Family education and counseling should be seen as essential in PTSD. These are the supportive tools that can help release some steam from the pressure cooker. Until we live in a culture in which grief is well understood and embraced, everyone needs basic grief education and structured support. This includes children. They can cope with that they know and have been taught, but they can never cope with what they don't know or what has been withheld from them. As for minimum age, I often say that any child old enough to love is old enough to mourn.

Family support groups run by a trained facilitator and with an education component help equip everyone in the family with the understanding and interpersonal skills they need to help themselves, each other, and the person with PTSD.

Here is what I wish every family struggling with PTSD understood: You have been injured by a traumatic event. It is normal for everyone who experienced the event—up close, especially—to be wounded in their hearts and souls. There is nothing wrong with any of you. However, you do have grief that needs to be expressed. Counselors can help all of you learn about grief and how to express it. Do not be ashamed. Do not despair. There is hope, and there is healing.

Obviously, certain days or times of the year will call out for much-needed support for the griever. For example, birthdays, holidays, the changing of seasons, and the anniversary of the event can all trigger griefbursts—heightened periods of sadness and loss that can be assuaged by ongoing support.

A vital part of the companioning role is to be among those whom the griever can depend upon to understand that grief's impact, especially in the aftermath of a traumatic event, continues long after society deems appropriate. Demonstrating this sensitivity in your responsiveness to the griever will reflect this awareness.

THE IMPORTANCE OF THE SIX CENTRAL NEEDS OF MOURNING

I cannot overemphasize the importance of how you, as a companion, can benefit from a working knowledge of these six needs of mourning. Essentially, facilitating them is your job description. As you follow the griever's lead in encountering these needs, providing a safe place for their expression and encouraging when appropriate, you will, over time, be privileged to witness the softening of the griever's symptoms.

Grief is real, and it does not simply go away as time passes. PTSD is a great example of the falsity of the adage, "Time heals all wounds." No, time alone does *not* heal all psycho-spiritual wounds, any more than time alone could heal a badly broken arm or a clogged artery. Companioning people through these six needs of mourning will give you the opportunity to be a catalyst for healing. Remember—grief waits on welcome, not on time!

CHAPTER NINE

The companioning philosophy of grief care

A number of years ago I realized that therapists needed a new model for caring for people experiencing grief. Client-centered talk therapy served as a good foundation, but I saw that truly effective grief counselors thought of grief in a more holistic and spiritual way. They did not see grief as a disorder or a disease but rather as a natural and necessary process. They also did not try to "cure" the grief of the people in their care; rather, they saw themselves as companions on the journey.

> "Compassion becomes real when we recognize our shared humanity."
>
> — PEMA CHODRON

I've always found it intriguing that the word "treat" comes from the Latin root word *tractare*, which means "to drag." If we combine that with "patient," we can really get in trouble. "Patient" means "passive long-term sufferer," so if we treat patients, we drag passive, long-term sufferers. Simply stated, that's not very empowering.

On the other hand, the word "companion," when broken down into its original Latin roots, means "messmate": *com* for "with" and *pan* for "bread." Someone you would share a meal with, a friend, an equal. I have taken liberties with the noun "companion" and made it into the verb "companioning" because it so well captures the type of counseling relationship I support and advocate. That is the image of companioning—sitting at a table together, being present to one another, sharing, communing, abiding in the fellowship of hospitality.

Companioning grievers is not about assessing, analyzing, fixing, or resolving another's grief. Instead, it is about being totally present to the griever, even being a temporary guardian of her soul.

The companioning model is anchored in the "teach-me" perspective. It is about learning and observing. In fact, the meaning of "observance" comes to us from ritual. It means not only to "watch out for" but also "to keep and honor," "to bear witness." The caregiver's awareness of this need to learn is the essence of true companioning.

Until now, PTSD has been primarily viewed as a disorder that requires treatment. So, the companioning model of caregiving, which sees the traumatized griever as the teacher, will be a dramatic shift for many caregivers who have been trained in the hierarchical medical-model approach. For the therapist, it requires giving up the ego-based identities of "doctor" or "expert." Ask yourself, challenge yourself—Can I do this?

If your desire is to support fellow human beings experiencing traumatic grief, you must create a "safe place" for people to embrace their feelings of profound loss. This safe place is a cleaned-out, compassionate heart. It is the open heart that allows you to be truly present to another human being's intimate pain.

As a grief caregiver, I am a companion, not a "guide"—which assumes knowledge of another's soul I cannot claim. To companion our fellow humans means to watch and learn. Our awareness of the need to learn (as opposed to our tendency to play the expert) is the essence of true companioning.

A central role of the companion to a griever is related to the art of honoring stories. Honoring stories requires that we slow down, turn inward and really listen as people acknowledge the reality of loss, embrace pain, review memories, and search for meaning.

The philosophy and practice of companioning interfaces naturally with hospitality. Hospitality is the essence of knowing how to live in society. Among the ancient Greeks, hospitality was a necessary element of day-to-day life. In a land where borders were permeable, it was important to get to know one's neighbors as potential friends. One way to do this was to share meals together. First, the guest and host would pour a libation to the gods. Then they would eat ("break bread") together. Then, after the guest was full, they would tell each other their stories, with the guest going first. Often, tears were shed as their stories were highly personal; battles, family, histories, and life tragedies all were a part of these stories. After the evening together, the host and guest were potential allies. Still today, oftentimes "breaking bread together" and then "telling personal stories" are key elements of companioning people in grief.

Henri Nouwen once elegantly described hospitality as the "creation of a free space where the stranger can enter and become a friend instead of an enemy." He observed that hospitality is not about trying to change people but offering them space where change can take place. He astutely noted that "hospitality is not a subtle invitation to adopt the lifestyle of the host, but the gift of a chance for the guest to find his own."

Also interesting to note is that the *Oxford English Dictionary* defines "companion" as "to accompany, to associate, to comfort, to be familiar with." This definition is actually illustrative of what it means to companion. In one sense, the notion is of comforting someone, which relates clearly to what a griever needs and deserves. In another sense, the notion is of knowing someone, being familiar with that person's experiences and needs; this notion clearly relates to the process of becoming familiar (being open to being taught by another), which can take place through the "telling of the story."

In sum, companioning is the art of bringing comfort to another by becoming familiar with her story (experiences and needs). To companion the grieving person, therefore, is to break bread literally or figuratively, as well as listen to the story of the other. Of course this may well precipitate tears and sorrow and tends to involve a give and take of story: I tell you my story and you tell me yours. It is a sharing in a deep and profound way.

The sad reality is that being a fellow companion in contemporary times seems to be a lost art. Many people (including trained mental health caregivers) may not know how to truly listen, really hear, and realize how to honor another person's story. I often say, "It's not so much what is new in grief care; it is what we lost that we once had."

ADVOCATING FOR THE COMPANIONING MODEL OF GRIEF CARE

A not-so-secret hope of mine is that the philosophical model of companioning grievers will eventually replace the medical model, which teaches that grief's goal is movement from illness to normalcy. The companioning philosophy empathizes

TREATMENT MODEL IN PTSD	COMPANIONING MODEL IN PTSD
The patient is sick/has a disorder.	The traumatized griever is having a normal and necessary response to an abnormal reality.
Understanding the brain's biochemistry will lead us to a cure.	Traumatic grief inhabits the soul and is fundamentally a spiritual journey.
Positions the traumatized griever in a passive role—the "patient."	Positions the traumatized griever in an active role—the mourner.
Control or stop painful symptoms. Distress is bad.	Express the symptoms and seek to learn from them. Distress is necessary and ultimately beneficial.
Follows a prescriptive model in which the caregiver is the expert.	The grieving person guides the journey. "Teach me" is the foundational principle.
Establish control. Create strategic plan of intervention.	Show up with curiosity and willingness to learn from the griever.
Grieving person ranges from compliant to non-compliant.	Grieving person expresses the reality of being "torn apart" as best he can.
Quality of care judged by how well the most obvious symptoms are "managed."	Quality of care monitored by how we allowed the griever to lead the the journey and facilitated active mourning.
The goal is an outwardly functional individual.	The goal is an individual who feels a new sense of wholeness, meaning, and purpose from the inside out and who lives and loves fully as part of a family system.

with the human need to mourn authentically without any sense of shame. The companioning model encourages every one of us to discover how loss forever changes us. The companioning model understands the normalcy of drowning in your grief before you tread water, and that only after treading water do you go on to swim. The companioning model helps the caregiver acknowledge the responsibility for creating conditions that allow the grieving person to journey through the wilderness that is grief.

In the world of professional PTSD care—which I believe is a subset of grief care, the companioning model has the potential to unlock new ways of understanding, communicating with, and helping the traumatized griever.

In the companioning model, complicated mourning, which includes traumatic grief, is perceived as blocked growth. In addition to possible treatment for intense fear-based symptoms, the traumatized griever needs help in understanding the six central needs of mourning and how to embrace them in ways that help him heal.

Most people are where they are in their grief journeys for one of two major reasons: 1) That is where they need to be at this point; or, 2) They need, yet lack, an understanding, safe place for mourning and a person who can help facilitate their work of mourning in more growth-producing, hope-filled ways. People with PTSD are almost always in the second group. When they come to you in the aftermath of a traumatic event, struggling with intense symptoms and having trouble functioning in their everyday lives, they need the support of someone who will normalize their experience and help them befriend the six central needs of mourning.

In essence, I believe that supporting people in grief is more of an art than a science. An artist fully embraces his or her own personal strengths and limitations to evolve a unique style that becomes a portrait of oneself as a caregiver and as a human being. I think it is a privilege to share my canvas with you, and I invite you to develop your own personal caregiver-as-artist way of being! Obviously, counseling models for supporting traumatized grievers can be viewed as portraits of the people who paint them. No two portraits are or should be exactly alike. As I uncover my portrait and share it with you, my hope is you will continue painting

THE TENETS OF COMPANIONING PEOPLE IN GRIEF

Following are 11 basic principles of companioning people who are grieving. They guide my caregiving. They apply to traumatized grievers and those experiencing any form of complicated grief as well as people experiencing normal grief.

TENET ONE
Companioning is about being present to another person's pain; it is not about taking away the pain.

TENET TWO
Companioning is about going to the wilderness of the soul with another human being; it is not about thinking you are responsible for finding the way out.

TENET THREE
Companioning is about honoring the spirit; it is not about focusing on the intellect.

TENET FOUR
Companioning is about listening with the heart; it is not about analyzing with the head.

TENET FIVE
Companioning is about bearing witness to the struggles of others; it is not about judging or directing these struggles.

TENET SIX
Companioning is about walking alongside; it is not about leading or being led.

TENET SEVEN
Companioning is about discovering the gifts of sacred silence; it is not about filling up every moment with words.

TENET EIGHT
Companioning is about being still; it is not about frantic movement forward.

TENET NINE
Companioning is about respecting disorder and confusion; it is not about imposing order and logic.

TENET TEN
Companioning is about learning from others; it is not about teaching them.

TENET ELEVEN
Companioning is about compassionate curiosity; it is not about expertise.

> "When we honestly ask ourselves which people in our lives mean the most to us, we often find it is those who, instead of giving advice, solutions, or cures, have chosen rather to share our pain and touch our wounds with a warm and tender hand."
>
> — HENRI NOUWEN

your own unique picture of what helps you companion people who have been impacted by traumatic events.

A REMINDER ABOUT THE ART OF EMPATHY

As a caregiver, you know that many nonprofessional people use the words "sympathy" and "empathy" interchangeably. Yet there is an important difference between the two—and you can leverage this difference to make yourself a better helper.

When you are sympathetic to someone else, you are noticing and feeling concern for his circumstances, usually at a distance. You're "feeling sorry" for him. You are feeling "pity" for him. You are looking at his situation from the outside, and you are acknowledging the distress passively. You may be offering a simple solution, platitude, or distraction. Sometimes sympathy also includes a touch (or a heavy dose) of judgment or superiority. Sympathy is "feeling for" someone else. For professional caregivers, sympathy is often a protective response to grief overload (too many grieving people with overwhelming loss experiences need help) and/or a professional distancing learned through medical-model training and organizational culture and requirements (diagnostic codes, treatment language, etc.).

Empathy, on the other hand, is about making an emotional connection. It is a more active process—one in which you try to understand and feel the other person's experience from the inside out. You are not judging the person or the circumstances. You are not offering simple solutions. Instead, you are making yourself vulnerable to the person's thoughts, feelings, and circumstances by looking for connections to similar thoughts, feelings, and circumstances inside you. You are being present and allowing yourself to be taught by the other person. Empathy is "feeling with" someone else.

From a grief caregiving standpoint, empathy normalizes. It welcomes. It creates a safe space. It builds the relationship between caregiver and griever. It assumes nothing but instead creates an opening for the traumatized griever to teach the caregiver what the experience is like for him.

EVASION-ENCOUNTER-RECONCILIATION

A vital helping role of the companion is attending to those thoughts, feelings, and behaviors that may be expressed by the griever. Then, being aware of those experiences, the companion's role is to enter into and empathetically respond in ways that assist the person in integrating the loss into a forever-transformed life.

What follows is a multidimensional model of the adult grief experience. A broad

	EVASION from the new reality	**ENCOUNTER** with the new reality	**RECONCILIATION** to the new reality
Grief characteristics	Shock Denial Numbness Disbelief	Disorganization, confusion, searching, yearning Generalized anxiety, panic, fear Physiological changes Explosive emotions Guilt, remorse, assessing culpability Loss, emptiness, sadness Relief, release	The capacity to organize and plan one's life toward the future
Primary needs of griever	Self-protection Psychological shock-absorber	Experience and expression of the reality of the loss Tolerate the emotional suffering	Remember the loss Develop a new self-identity Relate the loss to a context of meaning
Time course (specific times are difficult to to predict)	Weeks, potentially months (variable)	Many months, often years (variable)	No specific timeframe

outline of the model explored here is provided in the following chart. Please note that three broad classifications of grief, entitled EVASION-ENCOUNTER-RECONCILIATION, are provided along with a more detailed description of components of these experiences. By no means do I pretend that this model is all-inclusive; however, I do hope it supports you in your companioning efforts.

Not every person will experience each and every response described and certainly not in the order outlined. Some regression will occur along the way and, without doubt, some overlapping. Unfortunately, a human being's response to loss is never as uncomplicated as described by the written word.

The art of companioning reminds us that it is quite acceptable for grievers to be adrift rather than on some kind of "managed" course. A "hospitable" presence is about creating a free and open sacred space in which the griever can enter and become a friend. This is the dedicated presence of the companion, unhampered by judgments, no plan to fix or change the griever or impose personal projections.

In the Buddhist tradition, Avalokiteshavara (Sanskrit for "Lord who looks down") is the Buddha of compassion, whose name literally means "he who hears the cries of those in pain." A companioning presence requires listening from the heart and attending without the felt need to control or manage a fellow human being's grief. This demands an engaged focus that happens best when opening one's heart to the role of caring witness. It is certainly not about being a grief expert who claims superior knowledge of someone else's journey.

The companion bears witness without being distracted. The companion accepts thoughts and feelings without feeling a need to interpret or change thoughts and feelings. The companion genuinely cares about helping the traumatized griever meet his mourning needs.

We hope that the griever who is suffering in our presence discovers that it is all right to be confused, depressed, anxious, and out of control. She knows she will not be expected to "buck up" or efficiently "get on with life." She knows her pain will be seen as a necessary and normal response to loss and not as an illness or disorder.

We hope that the griever who is broken begins to feel safe in her psyche in this environment of unconditional love and empathy. She has discovered a companion who can be present to her in her darkness. Her brokenness can become visible as we companions "watch out for," "keep and honor," and "bear witness" to the transformative experience of grief.

Bodhichitta is a Sanskrit word meaning "noble or awakened heart." When you experience bodhichitta, you allow the pain and suffering of others to touch your heart and you turn it into compassion. Instead of pushing pain away, you open your heart and allow it to touch your "well of reception."

Authentic compassion happens when you accept the griever as an equal, all the while knowing there is nothing you can (or should) do to instantly relieve pain and suffering. While you are not responsible for curing the griever, you are being responsible for seeking to empathize and understand what the depth of the pain and suffering feels like. Then, as you companion your fellow human being, you resonate with the helping attitude that says, "Let us sit beside one another and explore this together. Allow me to be totally present to you as we bear witness to your special needs together." This collegial attitude of compassion serves to soften and purify your heart and brings you to a sacred space of unconditional love.

In the expression of this compassionate curiosity, the companion trusts that going fully into the dark opens the griever to the light. The paradox is that going further into the depths of suffering is what creates access to the hope of re-entering the light of a purpose-filled life. The companion does not have to rush healing or demand "resolution."

The companion stays present to what is without trying to treat it away or get the griever "over it." The companion provides a container in which even the most overwhelming times of darkness can be affirmed and survived. The companion is fully present because he brings a beginner's mind and is not attached to outcome.

The companion recognizes that releasing any and all urges to fix unlocks the capacity to be present to someone in the wilderness of grief. There is an awareness that when someone is suspended in the anguish of grief, appropriate care is not trying to get him back in control, but rather sitting with him in the dark. This takes large doses of humility—and humility is about accepting reality as it is without trying to outsmart or fix it.

I realize, of course, that some mental health caregivers might interpret the term "companioning" to be soft or exclusively philosophical. Yet in reality, it is practical. It requires the caregiver to learn specific helping skills to facilitate authentic mourning. If you are interested in learning more about the companioning philosophy of grief care, I suggest you read *Companioning the Bereaved: A Soulful Guide for Caregivers*. In that book I explore each of the 11 tenets of companioning in more depth, which will provide you with a solid foundation upon which to build your own philosophy of traumatic grief care. Also, my Center for Loss offers 150 hours of training resulting in a certificate (in affiliation with Colorado State University) that acknowledges the intensive study of a body of knowledge. That body of knowledge must then be translated from philosophical principles to clinical practice. One of the courses (30 hours) that comprise the certificate is specific to the application of the companioning model in PTSD.

CHAPTER TEN

When traumatic grief goes unmourned

When people carry their pain from life losses instead of mourning that pain, it comes back to haunt them. It keeps trying to get their attention until they give it the attention it demands and deserves. As Michel de Montaigne once observed, "The man who fears suffering is already suffering from what he fears."

"The frightening thing about loss is what we do to ourselves to avoid it. We know we cannot live without losing, but this knowledge does not prevent us from seeking to protect ourselves. So we narrow our souls. We draw ourselves tighter and tighter. No longer open to the world with all its hurts, we feel safe. By narrowing ourselves, though, we end up with more hurt than if we were free."

— DAVID WOLPE

When grief goes unexpressed, or unmourned, it destroys people's enthusiasm for life and living. It can deny them their creativity, gifts, and talents. The result is that these parts of themselves go stagnant or remain unclaimed inside of them, wanting to get out but feeling trapped. I often call it "living in the shadow of the ghosts of grief."

For traumatized grievers who have not been well companioned through mourning and who have not reconciled their traumatic loss experiences and subsequent grief fully, it is as if they have an imaginary cage surrounding them. In the cage are a multitude of potential symptoms that reveal that they are carrying the pain of grief. Trapped inside the cage, they are devoid of the desire to fulfill their life dreams, which is the very essence of creating a meaningful life and fulfilling their spiritual potential.

Following are some of the common fall-out symptoms I have observed in people who are living in the shadow of the ghosts of grief—both normal grief and traumatic grief—and have not had the opportunity or willingness to authentically mourn. A culture that too often labels grief symptoms as pathological, that shames people for openly mourning life losses, that is preoccupied with quick fixes for emotional pain, invariably ends up inviting people to carry grief.

SYMPTOMS OF CARRIED GRIEF

- Difficulties with trust and intimacy
- Depression and negative outlook
- Anxiety and panic attacks
- Psychic numbing and disconnection
- Irritability and agitation
- Substance abuse, addictions, eating disorders
- Physical problems, real or imagined

Now let's explore each of these symptoms a bit further.

Difficulties with trust and intimacy

People naturally fear what they do not know. I often think of how mourning requires a safe holding environment, a reliable sanctuary that is able to affirm all that we are and feel. When people experience loss but have not been provided with the safety and encouragement to mourn, their trust in people and the world around them is naturally compromised. In essence, they often fear intimacy and avoid closeness to others.

Many grief-carriers have taught me that they feel unlovable. Whether they attribute their self-esteem issues to unmourned losses or not, their brokenness makes them feel deficient or less-than. This can become, of course, a self-fulfilling prophecy. The grief-carrier may have an awareness of the need for love but at the same time feel unworthy of it. The reality is that this person feels unloved, and this translates into "I am unlovable." The tragic result is often isolation and loneliness. Some of these people do get married or attempt to have close relationships but still keep distance in an effort to stay safe.

In PTSD, as we have said, feelings of estrangement or detachment from others are considered a diagnostic symptom. What if we are able to treat away the glitchy and horrific memory-related problems with techniques such as EMDR...but we don't also help the traumatized griever truly embrace the pain, search for meaning, and develop a new-self-identity, all the while being supported and accepted by others? I believe that we're setting up this griever for ongoing difficulties with trust and intimacy...and carried grief.

Depression and negative outlook

In my experience, grief-carriers often present with what I call loss of their divine spark—that which gives purpose and meaning to our living. When their spirits remain muted, there is an ongoing hampering of the capacity to live life with meaning and purpose. The result is often depression and a negative, cynical view of life.

Depression symptoms include sadness, inactivity, difficulty with thinking and concentrating, a significant increase or decrease in appetite, sleep disturbance, feelings of hopelessness and dejection, and sometimes suicidal thoughts or actions. While there are multiple causes of depression, experience suggests that carried grief is a contributor for many people.

Depression sometimes masks itself as a general negative outlook on life. While some grief-carriers don't experience deep, dark depression, they suffer from a chronic, low-grade depression—dysthymia. The world begins to look gray. They lose their full range of emotional functioning, defending against ever being really happy or really sad. Sometimes they rationalize this mood state as "this is just what life is like."

Similarly, feelings of meaninglessness often pervade the lives of grief-carriers. People who grieve but don't mourn often feel isolated emotionally and lack a sense of meaning and purpose. They experience a sense of soullessness, or a loss of vitality and enthusiasm for life and living. They feel empty and alone.

Negativity is another diagnostic symptom of PTSD. Can we "fix it" with antidepressants or short-term cognitive behavioral therapy, for example? I don't think so. While antidepressants and CBT are sometimes both extremely effective components of treatment, any therapy that sees traumatic grief as a short-term problem or that attempts to get rid of a symptom without also exploring the causes of that symptom is setting up the person for ongoing problems.

Anxiety and panic attacks

Some grief-carriers struggle with a persistent and generalized anxiety. Anxiety is often reflected in motor tension (fatigue, muscle aches, easy startle response); autonomic hyperactivity (dry mouth, gastrointestinal distress, heart racing); apprehensive expectations (fears of injury or death); and hyper-vigilance and scanning (hyper-alertness, irritability, and problems with sleep disturbance). Again, just as with depression, there can be multiple causes of anxiety; however, I am certain that carried grief is a contributor for many people.

Anxiety sometimes shows up in the form of panic attacks. Panic is a sudden, overpowering fright. On occasion, these attacks may last for hours, though attacks are typically for a period of minutes, during which the person literally experiences terror. Panic attacks are often recurrent and episodic, though for some people they become chronic.

I have seen numerous people in counseling whose panic attacks were the doorway to get them to heed their carried grief and learn to authentically mourn. In helping people with PTSD, would it be useful to think of their fear and anxiety symptoms, which tend to be the attention-getters, as surface-level evidence of their deep psychic injury? What if we helped them mourn deeply and fully without immediately trying to treat away their fear? If we worked with them on normalizing the pain and searching for meaning, for example, would the fear naturally subside of its own accord?

Psychic numbing and disconnection

While shock and numbness are normal responses in the face of loss, some grief-carriers get so detached that they literally feel disconnected from the world around them. The result is that the world and the people in it seem unreal. Grief-carriers may live their days in a daze, going through the motions yet not feeling present to others and even themselves. Some people describe this as a dream-like state with feelings of unreality. They are existing but not really alive to what is going on around them. Short-term memory loss and confusion are often also a part of this experience.

Numbing results in a feeling of existing but not really living. The muting power of numbness prevents them from experiencing or sharing in even the positive things that may be going on around them.

While numbing symptoms (apart from avoidance) have been removed from the current DSM-approved presentation of PTSD, anyone who has worked with people with PTSD will tell you that they often present or self-describe as numb. They may also dissociate in an attempt to compartmentalize their injured selves from their still-functioning-but-flat selves.

Again I would ask: if you are able to treat away the fear-based symptoms but the person is left with ongoing feelings of numbness and disconnection, have you really helped her?

Irritability and agitation

Some grief-carriers express their pain indirectly through irritability and agitation. These symptoms may show up at work, at home, or anywhere they can find expression. It is like they are in a pressure cooker, and they are trying to release the pressure. In its extreme form, this symptom may show up as uncontrolled anger or rage.

These emotions of protest are often an unconscious attempt to fight off the underlying, more primary emotions of pain, helplessness, hurt, isolation, and aloneness. People around those exhibiting these emotions sense or experience their irritability and agitation and begin to avoid them, resulting in more carried pain and less authentic mourning.

Irritability and aggressive, self-destructive, and reckless behavior are expressly part of the DSM-5 PTSD picture. Would antidepressants help make a person with PTSD less irritable? Probably. Would Ativan calm his aggression? Possibly. Would either of these treatments actually help him understand, explore, and express the source of his emotions, however? No.

Substance abuse, addictions, eating disorders

Many grief-carriers will self-treat their pain through substance abuse, addictive behaviors, or eating disorders. Modern society provides an increasing number of substances that might be abused. People are usually abusive of or addicted to a specific substance, such as alcohol, cocaine, or food. However, grief-carriers can also be addicted to activities, such as destructive relationships, sex, smoking, gambling, gaming, porn, work, exercise, achievement, over-caretaking of others, religiosity, and materialism. These substances and activities are ways the person tries to distract himself from, deny, or dampen the pain of life losses.

According to the National Center for PTSD, more than twenty percent of veterans with PTSD are also substance abusers. Six of every 10 vets with PTSD smoke. And one in three vets who seeks treatment for substance abuse also has PTSD. The good news is that the ready availability of these statistics means that the link between PTSD and substance abuse is widely recognized. The potentially bad news is that once the substance abuse abates, the person may be considered "cured." While ongoing sobriety for people with PTSD who had been using is indeed a laudable step, it does not equate to "resolution" or, more importantly, reconciliation.

Physical problems, real or imagined

If we don't mourn one way, it comes out another. Many grief-carriers store the pain in their bodies. The result is that the immune system breaks down and illness surfaces. Many formal studies have documented significant increases in illness following the experience of a variety of losses in life, particularly death loss.

When we authentically mourn, these physical symptoms are normal and temporary. However, when people shut down, deny, or inhibit mourning, they sometimes assume a "sick role" in an effort to legitimize not feeling well to those around them. They somaticize their feelings of grief.

Sometimes the physical symptoms are very real; other times they are imagined. These imagined symptoms are often a silent voice crying out for the need to give expression to the carried pain. The imagined illnesses usually express themselves through multiple symptoms and complaints presented in a vague fashion. Typically, there are no organic findings to support a physical diagnosis.

The somaticizer may become so completely preoccupied with bodily involvement and sickness that she has little or no energy to relate to others and to do the work of mourning. Even in the absence of real illness and emotional support from medical caregivers, no amount of reassurance or logic convinces her that she is not physically sick. The unconscious need to protect herself requires that this person desperately needs the belief in illness to mask feelings connected to the loss and grief.

In addition to the fight-or-flight fear-response symptoms of shortness of breath, sweating, etc., physical symptoms such as chronic pain, headaches, stomach pain, dizziness, tightness in the chest, muscle cramps, and low back pain are often seen in PTSD. In fact, veterans who have been diagnosed with psychiatric conditions are significantly more likely than others to have risk factors for cardiovascular disease, like hypertension and diabetes.

While physical symptoms are not called out in the DSM-5 criteria for PTSD, they are commonly present. And like the other symptoms in this carried-grief discussion, they can be thought of as—in the absence of other physical etiology—indicators that something is wrong emotionally and spiritually. For people who have experienced a traumatic event, this "something" is often unmourned grief.

COMMON LIFE LOSSES

In thinking about carried grief and its cumulative effects, it's helpful to consider the various significant life losses we all encounter along the way.

LOSS OF PEOPLE YOU LOVE

- Separation (physical and/or emotional)
- Rejection
- Hostility/grudges
- Illness (such as Alzheimer's, debilitating conditions)
- Divorce
- Abandonment/betrayal
- Death
- Empty nest

LOSS OF PETS

LOSS OF ASPECTS OF SELF

- Self-esteem (often through physical, sexual, or emotional abuse or rape, humiliation, rejection, or neglect)
- Health, physical or mental ability

Job (downsizing, firing, failed business, retirement)

Control (such as through addiction, victimization)

Innocence (such as through abuse, exposure to immoral behavior)

Sexual identity/ability/desire

Security (such as through financial problems, war)

Expectations about how our lives should/would be

Reputation

Beliefs (religious, spiritual, belief in others we trusted)

Dreams (cherished hopes for the future)

LOSS OF PHYSICAL OBJECTS

Home (such as through a physical disaster, move or transition into assisted-living environments)

Linking objects (special items such as photos that carry emotional weight)

Money

Belongings (through theft or fire, etc.)

Nature/place (through a move, changing land use)

LOSS THROUGH DEVELOPMENTAL TRANSITIONS

Toddlerhood to childhood

Childhood to adolescence

Adolescence to adulthood

Leaving home

Marriage

Having/not having children

Mid-life

Taking care of parents

Retirement

Old age

Note that this list of common losses does not specifically broach the subject of traumatic losses. It is extremely common for people to present with symptoms of carried grief even when they have never suffered a trauma. Instead, significant but untraumatic losses build up over time, and if they are not mourned in real time as they occur, they accumulate into a heavy load of carried grief. On the flip side, traumatized grievers are almost always carrying some older, accumulated grief in addition to their traumatic grief—thus, even if the traumatic event was relatively recent, there is the potential need for catch-up mourning.

CHAPTER ELEVEN

Catch-up mourning for traumatic grief

In grief, the healing process is a continuum. It begins with the caregiver's (and the person's) awareness that the person is carrying unmourned grief, and it evolves to experiencing a meaning-filled life. And in between is the focus of this chapter: the healing process.

Healing carried grief does not happen by itself. Healing requires caregivers and the people they help to identify and befriend the carried pain. Both must openly acknowledge the presence of something important that deserves attention.

> **"A wound that goes unacknowledged and unwept is a wound that cannot heal."**
>
> — JOHN ELDREDGE

As I have said, time alone has nothing to do with healing. Healing requires active engagement with griefs. And even then, life losses are never "fixed" or "resolved"; they can only be soothed and integrated through actively experiencing and expressing the mixture of thoughts and feelings that arise.

Grief is like a spiral. Spirals are unending. You can go through the same circuit again and again, but traveling up the spiral, you pass through the same symptoms at a different level, experiencing a slightly different perspective each time. They do not form discrete, static shapes because spirals can always grow and change.

The gradual movement toward transformation invites emotional, spiritual, and interpersonal growth. With the support of a compassionate companion counselor, the person's capacity to reveal her losses and make deep and lasting changes becomes possible.

I have had the honor of working with hundreds of people who have allowed me to support them in mourning life losses that originate from carried pain. I use the term "catch-up mourning" to describe the process that helps them experience a more considered, conscious life, rather than just drifting in a fog or living out their carried pain.

A model I have created to help in the catch-up mourning process is outlined on page 112. The entire premise of helping my fellow human beings do catch-up mourning is my belief that when we learn to be with our pain that we have up until that point denied, we retrieve those parts of ourselves that were left behind. The result is that we are able to accept and integrate those parts of ourselves. We discover that in giving voice to our mourning lies the wisdom we need to live a meaningful, purposeful life. If we mourn our carried pain, we can truly and fully live until we die.

CATCH-UP MOURNING:

Going backward and giving attention to any grief you have carried from past losses in your life, including—and especially—any traumatic events. The purpose of going back and doing grief work is anchored in eventually freeing you to go forward with newfound meaning and purpose in your life, living, and loving.

In the broadest sense, deciding to recognize and encounter carried pain is a choice between opposites: a life devoid of deep feeling or a deeply felt life; escapist activities or meaningful activities. It means choosing between experiencing a life with its very real pains and pleasures or living in an anesthetized fog in which authentic feelings are inhibited; between a consciousness of our deepest feelings, or a vague, muted self-awareness. Giving attention to carried pain is, in many ways, choosing between living life from a place of truth or living a lie. When you are living a lie, you are misrepresenting the reality of your experience or the truth of your being. You are allowing a disconnect between the self that resides deep within you—your true self—and the self you manifest in the world around you.

For example, you are living a lie when you say you are angry but the truth is you are afraid. When you laugh but what you really need is to cry. When you present yourself as having values you do not feel or hold. When you pretend a love you do not feel. When you are kind to everyone except the people you claim to love. When you profess beliefs only to win acceptance.

When you end up living a lie, you are always your own first victim because the fraud is ultimately directed at yourself. If you are living a series of lies, you do so because you feel or believe that who you really are is not acceptable. You value a delusion in someone else's mind above your own knowledge of the truth. The result is living an incongruent life and experiencing the carried grief symptoms outlined on pages 102 through 107.

As I've said, our mourning-avoidant culture invites people to carry pain and encourages them to live an inauthentic life. People are often influenced in ways that make an appreciation of authentically mourning life losses all but impossible. We learn early in life to deny feelings of loss and to wear a mask, and eventually we lose contact with our inner selves. We become unconscious to much of our inner selves in adjusting to the world around us.

Significant adults in our childhoods often encouraged us to disown fear, grief, anger, and pain because such feelings made them uncomfortable. Adults who carry grief tend to raise children who carry grief, not only through direct communication, but through their own behavior, which models for the child what is appropriate, proper, and acceptable.

The paradox is that in order to live in this environment, we often learn to "play dead" as a way of making life more tolerable. Playing dead is so common for many grief-carriers that it becomes our perception of normal. It is the familiar, the comfortable; whereas living "alive" can feel strange, even disorienting. Sadly, playing dead is a recipe for self-rejection and self-estrangement. Those who live in the shadow of the ghosts of grief are among the many that I call the "living dead."

When we as caregivers honor the presence of people's current and carried grief, when we help them understand the need to surrender to the appropriateness of mourning their losses, we are helping them commit to facing the pain. We are committing ourselves to companion them as they experience their anguish in ways that allow them to begin to breathe life into their souls again.

In this book, I hope you find encouragement to help traumatized grievers gently befriend their carried grief. At first it often seems strange to them that they must make grief their friend. Instead of pulling down the blinds and shutting out light and love, you will invite them to come out of the darkness and into the light. Slowly, and with your help and companionship, they can and will return to life (or experience it deeply for the first time!) and begin living and loving in ways that put stars back into their skies.

A MODEL FOR CATCH-UP MOURNING

Because of our culture's grief avoidance and our concomitant medical-model's grief pathologizing, most of us, I believe, carry grief to some extent. Therefore, the model I describe below pertains to working with counseling clients with virtually any diagnosis, because carried grief is likely a contributor to their struggles. However, **people with PTSD are particularly susceptible to carried grief because PTSD is not yet formally recognized as a symptom of significant loss and therefore a grief response.**

HEALING CARRIED GRIEF: A FOUR-STEP MODEL

STEP 1: Acknowledging carried grief

STEP 2: Overcoming resistance to do the work

STEP 3: Actively mourning carried grief

STEP 4: Integrating carried grief

Simply put, grief requires mourning. And traumatic grief requires mourning that is as wide and as deep as the injury that created it. Many people with PTSD receive brief and shallow/"targeted" support when what they really need and deserve is open-ended, compassionate companionship that follows them where they lead.

Until the person with PTSD feels a renewed sense of wholeness, hopefulness, meaning, and joy in life (see signs of reconciliation on page 124), he remains a candidate for additional catch-up mourning.

STEP 1:
Acknowledging carried grief

Helping people with PTSD who, despite initial treatment for acute fear-based symptoms, are still experiencing life-dulling symptoms of carried grief (pages 102 through 107), begins with creating a safe place and process for them to begin to uncover and share their cumulative stories of loss and pain. (Of course, you must already have established a trusting relationship.)

While the companioning philosophy of caregiving champions the griever as expert of his own grief rather than the counselor, it's appropriate at this time to briefly educate the person in your care about the concepts of carried grief and catch-up mourning. After all, not only does our culture at large frown upon and deny grief and mourning, but **the dominant PTSD paradigm tends to reinforce the ideas of grief symptoms as abnormal and ideal treatment as fast and curative. Asking the person, at this point, to slow down and even go backward as he mines for unmourned losses may fly in the face of everything he has heretofore been told about PTSD.**

Beyond approaching your work with people who have PTSD with the heart and the mind of a companion counselor, I do not prescribe an ideal recipe of therapeutic techniques. In general, as I have said, I believe that talk therapy is essential to fostering mourning, especially catch-up mourning. Treatments such as psychopharmacological agents, cognitive processing, and exposure therapy as well as tools such as journaling, support group work, art therapy, and complementary therapies, may be selectively used *in addition to* talk therapy, but open-ended, client-focused talk therapy is the essential foundational tool. Sometimes experiential tools help people access the unconscious processes, thoughts, feelings, and memories that otherwise remain hidden from ordinary awareness, which in turn allows them to be explored in talk therapy.

And while methods that focus on the expression of feelings as the end goal of the healing work are beneficial, I believe the preferred approach is to combine emotional release with cognitive insight. In my experience, the best verifying evidence that people are on the right path to healing is increasing recognition and clarity of their feelings, which is the result of both insight and connection to their emotions. But always keep in mind that authentic catch-up mourning demands not just thinking but feeling. Authentic healing cannot take place in the context of intellectual insight in isolation. In other words, people sometimes experience a wealth of insight without integrating their deeper feelings. True healing of carried pain is ultimately an emotional and spiritual journey with insight only serving as a road map.

STEP 2: Overcoming resistance to do the work

Approaching feelings that have been inhibited or denied can be a naturally difficult experience. When people first begin to feel some intense emotions surrounding their carried grief, they may fear that their pain will be limitless. Many people I have helped over the years have told me some variation on, "If I let myself start to feel, I may never stop." However, opening the door to carried pain, while often frightening, is necessary in the healing process.

Obviously, to begin to admit to having such frightening and powerful emotions undermines any denial that one is "just fine." And remember, many people around the griever, and society in general, would prefer it if she were "just fine." Sometimes when people start to do catch-up mourning, some people in their lives will label them as having problems or becoming emotionally unstable.

In fact, what they are actually doing is openly acknowledging the presence of something important that deserves their attention. Each step in this process requires grievers' courage to refuse to give in to their fears. Still, they may be tempted to take the path of least resistance, to return to their defenses and ignore the feelings within that are inviting them to acknowledge and honor them.

Yes, honor them. Honoring literally means "recognizing the value of and respecting." To honor their emotional and spiritual selves is not self-destructive or harmful; it is self-sustaining and life-giving.

Grievers must set their intention to mourn carried grief. Having intention is defined as being conscious of what you want to experience. When they set their intention to heal unhealed wounds, they make a true commitment to positively influence the work that must be done. Essentially, they choose between living an unlived, often miserable life or becoming an active participant in their catch-up mourning.

Their decision to heal is a moment-by-moment, day-by-day choice. They take one small step forward, they commit to one particular action, and then they take the next step. By saying yes in the moment, they gradually create momentum toward their healing: "Yes, I will share one untold part of my story today."

Grievers who are able to see themselves as the center of their own healing process and are able to make choices that will serve them well in the long-term find it easier to make the commitment to heal. Realizing that they are in control, that they will not be forced to do anything against their will, is critical to their feeling safe as they do their work. Paradoxically, when they are assured that their, "No, I'm not ready" will be respected, they experience the unfolding of being able to one day say, "Yes, I am ready."

Being in control of dosing their unmourned pain is the opposite of what happened when the traumatic event occurred. Now they can make choices. Reliving painful feelings and taking risks are part of the healing process. But their desire to make choices lets them ask themselves, "Is this the right time? Am I willing to go through this now? Do I want to open up to my carried pain, or do I want to shut down and continue to live in the shadow of the ghosts of grief?"

I have asked people with carried grief to commit to this step of the catch-up mourning process in writing. Here is how one person expressed the decision to mourn her carried grief:

> *I have decided to pay attention to my inner pain, to feel the feelings I've tried to stuff inside. I don't want to keep living the way I have been. I am going to choose the truth and free myself to discover peace in my heart. I have the strength and desire to explore my losses in more depth and mourn them so that I can free myself to live with new meaning and purpose in life.*

The nice thing about creating a written statement such as this one is that this person can then refer back to this statement as she does her work of mourning. When she needs motivation, she re-reads her commitment and continues with her journey toward healing.

As a companion counselor, your role during this step of the process is to affirm the normalcy of the person's reticence and to allow him to set the pace even as you encourage him to commit to facing and even embracing the carried pain. So, affirm the natural resistance, but gently urge the person to go forward with courage and commitment.

STEP 3: Actively mourning carried grief

Actively mourning carried grief is the most painful step toward reconciling carried grief, but also the most liberating. On the one hand, embracing carried pain from life losses naturally brings sorrow. On the other hand, I have seen that the discovery that it is never too late to mourn creates the energy to actually do the work necessary to heal and create a meaning-filled life.

Our feelings are the way in which we perceive our existence. They are a vital link in our relationship to others, ourselves, and the world around us. They are how we know we are alive. That is why when we shut our feelings down, we risk being among the living dead. When we disconnect ourselves from our true feelings, we have no true awareness of life. But when we stop to identify and experience our feelings, both current and long-buried, we wake up.

To actively mourn their carried grief, the people who come to us for help need permission, validation, and the space in which to safely feel. They need *sanctuary*, which is a place of refuge from external demands. A space where they are free to disengage from the outside world. A place where their need to turn inward and suspend will not be hurried or ridiculed. As a compassionate grief companion, you have the privilege to provide that sanctuary and, with empathy, allow them to open the door wide as you follow them inside.

Once the atmosphere of sanctuary is established, a central role of the compassionate companion is the art of honoring life stories surrounding loss. To honor people's stories requires that you proceed slowly and really listen as they acknowledge the reality of their losses, review memories, and discover meaning in their continued living. Companion counselors realize that people who are carrying grief must go backward and give attention to their cumulative losses before they can go forward.

I do not pretend that openly mourning carried losses, especially traumatic losses, is done easily and efficiently. Many people have carried pain for years, and when traumatic grief is added to the scales, it can feel like they tip beyond all righting. But because PTSD is recognized as a legitimate diagnosis and is eligible for reimbursable treatment (finally, an upside to the medicalization of traumatic grief!), people who are fortunate enough to receive ongoing care based on the companioning philosophy and the catch-up mourning model will indeed learn to actively mourn their carried grief, and many will achieve the kind of deep and lasting healing of their traumatic injury that only active, thorough mourning can accomplish.

I believe deep in my soul that a blessing we all instinctively seek in mourning our life losses is not to live in the absence of pain. It is to live "alive" in a way in which our pain has meaning. To search for and discover this meaning in our current buck-up culture, we need compassionate companions—grief caregivers like you who do not perceive the thoughts and feelings of grief as inappropriate or a "disorder" but instead see them as a necessary and normal response to significant loss.

Compassionate companions are willing and able to help people with carried pain and give attention to the causes behind their symptoms. Companion counselors are very sensitive to the consequences that carried pain can have. They activate their natural empathy and unconditional love as they help those in their care gain an understanding of how their symptoms of carried pain are a natural *result* of their life injuries rather than an illness unto themselves.

For me, compassionate companions are also those caregivers who have explored their own history of life losses and had the courage to do the work of their own authentic mourning. This process forges their integrity and tends to disengage the need to exercise power over their clients. Only when compassionate companions have done their own mourning work are they able to provide the people in their care with the perspective they need to experience and express their own loss history. In addition, companion counselors recognize they have an obligation to the people in their care to stay present to them as the catch-up mourning experience unfolds. In other words, companion counselors serve as a bridge to getting people the resources they need to do their work of mourning.

I recognize that becoming and remaining a companion counselor in this era of grief and PTSD medicalization is not easy. Many trained mental health caregivers were never taught how to truly listen, really hear, and honor stories of loss. And some organizations that employ caregivers or reimburse care see the companioning philosophy of grief care as so much hokum. These organizations are likely to be attracted to treatments that attempt to quickly and efficiently eradicate symptoms. But if you have ever looked into the eyes (and souls) of people with PTSD and thought, "These people are so deeply injured. They deserve more substantive care," then you recognize the need for a reframing of PTSD and a new way of helping its sufferers. Yes, you, too, can be a "responsible rebel."

THE NEEDS OF MOURNING IN CARRIED GRIEF

Here I would like to briefly revisit the six central needs of mourning, because it is these same six needs that grief-carriers must actively work to meet if they are to truly and deeply heal their psychic injuries. In other words, the six needs are "how" grief-carriers mourn their carried grief and begin to achieve reconciliation.

MOURNING NEED 1: Acknowledge the reality of the loss(es)

Traumatized grievers typically need some guidance and modeling in acknowledging both the many primary and secondary losses created by the traumatic event but also considering past losses in their lives that may be contributing to their PTSD symptoms. Some people can easily name their griefs, while others struggle to do so. Of course, this makes sense. Identifying carried griefs can be very difficult, particularly ones that may have been denied or "stuffed" for years.

Spending time in the beginning uncovering all significant unmourned losses helps people become aware of the cumulative nature of grief. On the other hand, when people in your care clearly want to focus on a particular loss, follow their lead. As their stories unfold and your relationship strengthens, you will be able to circle back and help them consider the effects of other life losses that weren't identified at first.

MOURNING NEED 2:
Feel the pain of the loss(es)

Authentic mourning creates what is called *perturbation*, which is "the capacity to experience change and movement." The word *feeling* originates from the Indo-European root that literally means "touch." So, it is embracing, or touching, their feelings that activates people's natural capacity to be touched and changed by the experiences they encounter along life's path. Simply put, emotions need motion.

The "stuck-ness" of PTSD is actually a symptom that people are not experiencing the change created by the loss. It's as if they've been broadsided but have not allowed themselves to reel from the impact, examine the wound, and move down the paths that lead to healing. Instead, they are still stuck at the moment of impact, like a paused video. They are not experiencing the necessary movement, or perturbation. This is not a disorder but rather an indication of the need for the expression of symptoms, thoughts, and feelings.

Each time people experience and integrate some of their carried pain, they gain confidence in their capacity to regroup after a period of emotional and spiritual work with you as their companion. Slowly, and with no rewards for speed, they come to discover that their denied grief does not overwhelm them. In the presence of unconditional love, they discover that they can allow these feelings to be experienced but still survive them.

MOURNING NEED 3:
Remember the loss

I spent some time discussing the issue of traumatic loss memories on pages 79 through 81. This mourning need, I think, can be the trickiest to help traumatized grievers meet. As they do their catch-up mourning, how much remembering is necessary? How much is too little? How much is too much?

While I believe that sharing memories is almost always essential, and the PTSD research affirms the effectiveness of treatments that in one way or another put memories of the traumatic event on the table, the companion counselor allows the unique person to take the lead. You might find that as your relationship develops and trust in the process grows, the person who was initially reticent to share memories may develop the confidence to open up.

MOURNING NEED 4: Develop a new self-identity

As a companion counselor, you will help people consider how their self-identities have been impacted by their life losses and carried grief. In acknowledging some painful aspects of their changed self-identities, they can mourn and sometimes release them. For example, some people with PTSD who knowingly or unknowingly continue to see themselves as victims may go on to release their feelings of victimization and embrace more empowering concepts of self-identity.

Many catch-up grievers also discover that as they work on this need, they ultimately discover some positive aspects of their changed self-identities. They often develop a renewed confidence in themselves and a more caring, kind, and sensitive self-image.

MOURNING NEED 5: Searching for meaning

The search for meaning is often the centerpiece of the catch-up mourning process. Even though there are not always answers to the difficult meaning-of-life-and-loss questions, people ultimately find value—and even peace—in wrestling with them. Also, the process of searching for meaning in loss is life-long. Like grief, it does not ever truly end. But people can achieve a peace in their search that allows them to live and love fully and to step out of the shadow of the ghosts of grief and into the light.

MOURNING NEED 6: Receive ongoing support from others

Grief-carriers, especially traumatized grief carriers, need companion counselors to support them for the long haul. That's where you come in. But people with PTSD also need the ongoing support of others in their lives to move forward in wholeness. I encourage people to involve those they love in their struggles with reconciling their carried grief. Those closest to them deserve their honesty and they, in turn, deserve the support of their friends and family.

Opening up to significant others, children, parents, siblings, and best friends about their awakening will help all these people understand the transformation the griever is undergoing. It will also help these people embrace the new person the griever is becoming.

I also urge grief-carriers who are so inclined to seek ongoing support from a support group, a spiritual leader, or others. Traumatized grievers can also often offer support to fellow grief-carriers.

SUPPORT GROUPS AND STORIES

As they actively mourn their carried grief in the company of a companion counselor, people can often be greatly helped by participating in a support group. The worth of these programs certainly does not emanate from empirically supported treatments but rather from something much more simple (yet powerful): the telling of stories.

The meetings are anchored in honoring each member's stories of grief and supporting each other's need to authentically mourn. No effort is made to interpret or analyze. The group affirms the storyteller for the courage to express the raw wounds that often accompany loss. The stories speak the truth. The stories create hope. The stories create healing.

Effective leaders of such groups come to recognize that their role is not so much about group counseling techniques as it is about creating "sacred space" in the group so that each person's story can be non-judgmentally received. Effective grief group leadership is a humble yet demanding role of creating this space in ways that members can express their wounds in the body of community. The very experience of telling one's story in the common bond of the group counteracts the isolation and shame that characterize so many people's lives in a mourning-avoidant culture. And, because stories of love and loss take time, patience, and unconditional love, they serve as powerful antidotes to a modern society that is all too often preoccupied with getting people to "let go" and "move on."

In the Canadian military, the Operational Stress Injury Social Support program, or OSISS, deploys screened, trained, and paid peers who have suffered from operational stress injuries to help one another through, essentially, the sharing of stories as well as general social support. The program, which includes one-on-one as well as group components, has found that veterans benefit from this approach because they a) all understand the military schema and share similar experiences, b) engage more deeply with care when they are playing an active (versus passive) role, and c) can act as role models for one another, fostering hope. It's a win-win for everyone involved, including the professional caregivers who oversee the program, because they learn more deeply about the veteran culture and what works.

The creation of new meaning and purpose in life requires that grievers "re-story" their lives. Obviously, this calls out for the need for empathetic companions, not treaters. Indigenous cultures acknowledge that honoring stories helps reshape a person's experience. The stories are reshaped not in the telling of the story once or twice or even three times, but over and over again. Grievers need compassionate listeners to hear and affirm their truths. So, as a companion, your upholding of people's stories allows you the privilege of being a "shapeshifter"!

The many benefits of honoring the stories of our fellow human beings include

- We can search for wholeness among our fractured parts.
- We can come to know who we are in new and unexpected ways.
- We can explore our past and come to a more profound understanding of our origins and our future directions.
- We can tentatively explain our view of the world and come to understand who we are.
- We can explore how love experienced and love lost have influenced our time on earth.
- We can discover that a life without story is like a book without pages—nice to see but lacking in substance.
- We can seek forgiveness and be humbled by our mortality.
- We can determine how adversity has enriched our meaning and purpose in life.
- We can journey inward and discover connections previously not understood or acknowledged.

- We can create an awareness of how the past interfaces with the present and how the present ebbs back into the past.
- We can discover that the route to healing lies not only in the physical realm but also in the emotional and spiritual realms.
- We can find that the fulfillment of a life well lived is bestowed through the translation of our past into experiences that are expressed through the oral or written word.
- We can come to understand that in our pain and suffering lies the awareness of the preciousness of each day on the earth.
- We can discover our truth in this present moment of time and space.

HONORING OUR OWN STORIES

I believe that grievers can instinctively sense who can listen to their stories and who cannot. They often look for signs of open-heartedness and will gladly tell their stories to those they sense have a receptive spirit. The capacity to attend to your own stories of loss allows you to open your heart and connect to other people's stories.

Honoring stories, both our own and others', requires that we slow down, turn inward, and create the sacred space to do so. Yes, this can be challenging in a fast-paced, efficiency-based culture in which many people lack an understanding of the value of telling the story. Yet, companions realize that it is in having places to re-story their lives that they can embrace what needs to be embraced and come to understand that the human spirit prevails. We heal ourselves as we tell the tale. This is the awesome power of story.

STEP 4: Integrating carried grief

When people have given attention to their carried grief in ways that it deserves and demands, they begin to experience a renewed sense of wholeness. To heal in grief literally means "to become whole." The key to integration of grief is to make connections and keep making them as people learn to continue their changed lives with fullness and meaning. While they have been irrevocably shaped by their losses, they now begin to understand that they do not have to be defined by those losses.

Traumatized grievers have often been anchored for a long time in their fear and carried grief. But as they actively mourn, they find they can once again begin to live authentically and honestly with themselves and those around them. As their new lives unfold, they reconnect with parts of themselves that had been left behind and discover new parts of themselves that they didn't recognize before. They start having more fun and relaxing into the joy of being alive. Life broadens. They have longed to be free and now realize they are. They have accepted responsibility for their healing and actively worked to make it so.

In grief, unlike in the medical world, healing is a holistic concept that embraces the physical, cognitive, emotional, social, and spiritual realms. Note that healing is not the same as curing, which is a medical term that means "remedying" or "correcting." You cannot remedy carried grief, but you can reconcile it. You cannot undo old injuries, but you can heal them.

Reconciliation is a term I find more appropriate for what occurs as people do the work of catch-up mourning of carried grief. With reconciliation comes new life energy and the capacity to be optimistic about their life journeys and to engage in the activities of being fully alive.

Reconciliation allows them to relax into the world around them. Reconciliation is not about "closure" but about "opening": opening further; learning more; connecting with the depths of their life losses; and becoming more loving, kind, and compassionate people. Instead of being among the living dead, they are awake, alive, and hope-filled.

A question: Would you say that you witness reconciliation in the people with PTSD in your care after completion of the treatments you currently employ? Or does their progress typically fall short of reconciliation as I have described it? Please don't think I am pointing fingers. I realize and understand that many compassionate caregivers' hands are tied when it comes to treatment planning and duration. Instead, I ask the question to highlight the sometimes dramatic difference between the outcomes of the companioning approach to grief care and the medical-model approach. The former is concerned with lifelong self-actualization, while the latter focuses on immediate symptoms relief.

I'm reminded of a quote from a book entitled *Patience: The Art of Peaceful Living*, by Allan Lokos. (Note that *dukkha* is a Buddhist term for uncomfortable feelings such as stress, discomfort, anxiety, and grief.)

> *To extinguish a fire we don't throw water on the flames, we throw water on what is burning. Fire exists because a fuel (wood, paper) has been heated to a point where it becomes combustible. To put out the fire we must cool the fuel so that it can no longer burn. The same is true of extinguishing* dukkha. *We cool the fuel, which, in the case of* dukkha, *is the causes and conditions that bring about suffering. In other words, we do what is necessary to change that which causes* dukkha. *Thus, we stop bringing about our unhappiness.*

Likewise, reconciling traumatic grief requires cooling not the symptoms but instead the causes and conditions that created the grief. We cannot erase loss as if it never happened, however, so we must acknowledge, embrace, and express it, which is the process that cools it.

CHAPTER TWELVE:

Where to go from here?

It was psychotherapist and spiritual thinker Thomas Moore who observed, "Our science and technologies approach life as a problem to be solved." Similarly, our medical model approaches traumatic grief as a pathology to be cured.

My hope is that you are now rethinking how best to support traumatized grievers. To experience and embrace the pain of loss is just as much a part of life as to experience the joy of love. Thoughts, feelings, and behaviors that naturally and necessarily result from significant loss are impossible to treat away with medical-model therapies. Instead, what they need and deserve is intensive care of the soul.

> **"Before we can gain the ability to feel for another person, we need to feel for ourselves, to sit with our own woundedness and brokenness until it becomes spiritual."**
>
> — TIAN DAYTON

But where do we go from here? As I write this, hundreds of millions of people the world over are suffering from traumatic grief. The companioning philosophy of care I advocate would match each of these people up with a companion counselor who would walk beside them through the long and recursive journey that is grief and help them step through the reconciliation needs of catch-up mourning.

But, I realize, we lack resources. There aren't enough companion counselors out there—therapists and laypeople who understand the normalcy and necessity of grief and mourning after loss. There isn't enough healthcare coverage. Our cultures create more trauma than there are healing resources to assuage it.

Still, I take up the charge advocated by Gandhi when he famously said, "Be the change you wish to see in the world." Every day I speak, write, teach, and counsel about grief and mourning both to caregivers and to laypeople, sharing the message that grief is a natural response to loss and that expressing grief—mourning—is the way to healing. Similarly, this book is my attempt to reach out to the PTSD community and get the change conversation going.

I don't have all the answers. But I do have some suggestions:

Talk to your colleagues about the concept of PTSD as traumatic grief.

If my stance in this book resonates with you even a little, consider sharing the book with your colleagues. Then schedule a lunch or in-service to talk about the idea of PTSD as a form of grief and how that idea might shift your organization's thinking or treatment strategies.

In larger organizations (like the VA) and in thoroughly medicalized mental health care groups (like psychiatry), rethinking PTSD as traumatic grief and treatment as mourning will not happen quickly or easily, if at all. This is not to say, of course, that there aren't many empathetic individuals within those organizations who understand the deeply spiritual nature of loss, grief, and mourning. But the organizations themselves are built upon numbers, scientific methods, and evidence-based thinking. Of them, all I am asking is to acknowledge the normalcy of grief and to consider grief's role and trajectory in PTSD. I also hope that they will entertain the possibility that grief's expression—mourning—creates a path to a deeper and richer kind of healing than any pill or short-term therapy ever could.

Talk to the people in your care about their grief.

If you're used to focusing on their symptoms—anxiety, withdrawal, numbing—and talking to them using clinical terminology, try opening up a dialogue that uses more open-ended, higher-level words like "grief" and "soul." See what happens.

Also, consider dropping language about disease, illness, and disorder when you talk to traumatized people in your care and instead use the language of injury and a normal response to an abnormal reality. Again, see what happens.

Find ways to foster peer support.

As I said (and as you've probably been thinking the whole time as you read this book), there aren't enough of us professional counselors to provide long-term therapy to all the millions of traumatic grievers in the world. The good news is that those millions of traumatic grievers can help one another, if only we provide them structure and mentoring.

Peer support groups provide a safe place for traumatized grievers to share their stories of loss and affirm the normalcy of what they are experiencing. The sharing that naturally unfolds in a support group helps grievers begin to meet all six of the needs of mourning, if you think about it. Ideally group members gather in person, but online groups can also be effective. Support groups for family members are also a great idea.

Peer counseling is another possibility—one that has been successfully implemented in several places across the country, such as the PFC Joseph Dwyer PTSD Peer-to-Peer Counseling program in New York state. In my many years as a grief educator, I have met hundreds of dedicated and passionate laypeople who, with a little professional guidance, can skillfully and, more important, compassionately companion fellow grievers. Those who have begun to achieve reconciliation themselves are usually at a point where they can help others.

Other options include traumatic grief conferences that bring together area grievers once a year, layperson-run phone hotlines, a drop-in community-center room specifically for traumatized grievers (rather like the VFW, but for everyone, not just vets), and a layperson-moderated online forum.

Integrate the six needs of mourning into your therapy programs.

The six needs of mourning (pages 75 through 87) are how we heal when we are in grief. Do your current therapy programs integrate all six of the needs? Are you providing opportunities for people to search for meaning? Are you allowing them to not only receive support from you but to support one another? The more deeply your programs incorporate all six of the needs of mourning, the more you will help traumatized grievers.

What's more, I believe you should consider explicitly teaching people in your care about the six needs of mourning. First of all, people often don't understand the difference between grief and mourning. When they first learn about the distinction, they often remark, "Oh! So I need to *express* my grief?" This small but critical key empowers them to start doing something about their injury. Then when they learn there are six distinct needs they need to meet, they often find that the structure organizes their understanding of all the chaotic thoughts and feelings they have swirling inside them.

Integrate the concept of carried grief and catch-up mourning into your therapy programs.

The people with PTSD in your care are likely carrying grief not only from the traumatic event they survived but also from earlier life losses. In fact, their "pre-existing" carried grief probably made them more susceptible to PTSD in the first place, because carried grief often indicates family-of-origin issues with emotional openness, personality characteristics that encourage "stuffing," and/or cultural and religious backgrounds that have inculcated "strength" and "forgiveness."

Inventorying past losses as well as the myriad secondary losses that emanated from the traumatic event will give both you and them the complete carried-grief picture. From there you can look together at life patterns that may be exacerbating the PTSD and find ways to mourn other significant unmourned losses.

Explore your own grief and mourning.

Earlier in this book I briefly mentioned that companion counselors must inventory their own carried grief and work through their own catch-up mourning in an effort to live as wholly and authentically as possible but also to prepare themselves to help other grief carriers as much as possible. As the saying goes, "You can never take anyone further than you go yourself."

Companion counselors offer themselves to the relationship with those in their care with a cleaned-out heart. It is the open heart that allows you to be truly present to another human being's intimate pain.

Receive training in the companioning method of grief care.

I wrote my tenets of companioning grievers, which had long guided me but had before then never been codified in writing, a number of years ago. Since that time, I've been honored that many people have encouraged me to teach more about these principles. There is now an international network of thousands of people who have trained with me in the companioning philosophy of caregiving to people in grief. In fact, several hundred North American hospice programs as well as a number of organ procurement organizations and the Tragedy Assistance Program for Survivors (TAPS) use the companioning philosophy as their foundational grief-care model. In courses I teach such as "Comprehensive Bereavement Skills Training" and "Companioning the Mourner: From Theory to Practice," caregivers learn to marry their previous training with the companioning philosophy and return to their organizations or practices prepared to hit the ground running, as it were. I am also now offering a course called "Companioning the Traumatized Griever: Reframing PTSD as Catch-Up Mourning." In addition to teaching courses at the Center for Loss, I travel to many places across North America each year to offer staff in-services on these and other topics.

What's more, graduates of my trainings live and work around the world—some of whom may practice near you. If you call my office at 970.226.6050, we would be happy to try to put you in touch with grief companions in your area who might be willing to serve as mentors, consultants, or sounding boards.

A final word

My hope is that you agree that it is time to face the need for change in how we think about and "treat" PTSD. If I have convinced you that PTSD is not a disorder but rather a type of complicated grief, one I call "traumatic grief," and if you believe that grief is not an illness but a normal and necessary response to the injury of loss, then we are on the same page and can begin to find ways to integrate the needs of mourning and the companioning philosophy into PTSD programs everywhere.

Companioning depends on our willingness to reject grief as a pathology and not think of our role as eradicating emotional and spiritual suffering. We must surrender to the wilderness that is traumatic grief to be willing to wander into the mystery. We have to expect chaos, confusion, disorder, and even despair. So-called "negative" emotions and experiences are not dangerous. Messiness has its place. Grief always start with confusion. We can't be companions if we refuse to be confused. Integration of loss often occurs in the space of not knowing. We don't need to be joined at the head with a mourner; we need to be joined at the heart.

At the very heart of companioning is the need to acknowledge the people in our care as equals. The power structure of "doctor" or "therapist" and "patient" or "client" is not only untenable, it's harmful. What makes us equals is that we are all human beings who will come to know the pain and suffering that result from the many losses we encounter in life. Those who experience traumatic events—and as we reviewed, there are millions of us—are especially able to help each other.

Companioning is also about compassionate curiosity. When we support each other with this humility, we open our hearts to another human being. Curiosity encourages us to take off our professional masks and create sacred, hospitable free space for traumatized grievers. It takes time and conscious effort to create this space in a mourning-avoidant culture. Compassionate curiosity encourages us to extend ourselves rather than withdraw into our professional training and distancing. Yes, companioning invites us to extend ourselves, open our hearts wide, be still, and really observe, witness, and listen.

I dream of a day when the term PTSD will be abandoned and all traumatized grievers will, without judgment or delay, receive the emotional and spiritual intensive care they need. I dream of a day when our culture will regard dark emotions as healthy and necessary, and grief as the bittersweet byproduct—the good fortune, even—of love and connection. While I'm honored that the companioning model is already taught at a number of universities, including in China, I dream of a day when the art of companioning people through traumatic grief will be taught in all universities and practiced universally.

It was Walt Disney who said, "All our dreams can come true, if we have the courage to pursue them." This book is what resulted when I mustered the courage to say what I have been thinking for some time about the grief most people call PTSD. I hope that you, in return, will have the courage to let me know what you think about my rabble-rousing—whether your reaction is good, bad, or indifferent.

What is *your* dream for the future of PTSD diagnosis and treatment? I hope we can work together to create positive change.

To contact Dr. Wolfelt about speaking engagements or training opportunities with his Center for Loss and Life Transition, email him at DrWolfelt@centerforloss.com.

Companioning the Bereaved
A Soulful Guide for Caregivers

This book by one of North America's most respected grief educators presents a model for grief counseling based on his "companioning" principles.

For many mental healthcare providers, grief in contemporary society has been medicalized—perceived as if it were an illness that with proper assessment, diagnosis, and treatment could be cured.

Dr. Wolfelt explains that our modern understanding of grief all too often conveys that at bereavement's "end" the mourner has completed a series of tasks, extinguished pain, and established new relationships. Our psychological models emphasize "recovery" or "resolution" in grief, suggesting a return to "normalcy."

By contrast, this book advocates a model of "companioning" the bereaved, acknowledging that grief forever changes or transforms the mourner's world view. Companioning is not about assessing, analyzing, fixing, or resolving another's grief. Instead, it is about being totally present to the mourner, even being a temporary guardian of his soul. The companioning model is grounded in a "teach me" perspective.

"This outstanding book should be required reading for each and every grief provider. Dr. Wolfelt's philosophy and practice of caregiving helps us understand we don't need to be joined at the head with the mourner, we need to be joined at the heart."

— A GRIEF COUNSELOR

ISBN 978-1-879651-41-8
191 pages • hardcover • $29.95

Companion
PRESS

All publications can be ordered by mail from:

Companion Press
3735 Broken Bow Road
Fort Collins, CO 80526
Phone: (970) 226-6050
Fax: 1-800-922-6051
www.centerforloss.com

Companioning the Dying
A Soulful Guide for Caregivers

By Greg Yoder
Foreword by Alan D. Wolfelt. Ph.D.

If you work with the dying in your career or as a volunteer, or if you are a family member or friend to someone who is dying, this book presents you with a caregiving philosophy that will help you know how to respond, and what to do with your own powerful emotions. Most of all, this book will help you feel at peace about both your own role as caregiver and the dying person's experience—no matter how it unfolds.

Based on the assumption that all dying experiences belong not to the caregivers but to those who are dying—and that there is no such thing as a "good death" or a "bad death," *Companioning the Dying* helps readers bring a respectful, nonjudgmental presence to the dying while liberating them from self-imposed or popular expectations to say or do the right thing.

Written with candor and wit by hospice counselor Greg Yoder (who has companioned several hundred dying people and their families), *Companioning the Dying* exudes a compassion and a clarity that can only come from intimate work with the dying. The book teaches through real-life stories that will resonate with both experienced clinical professionals as well as laypeople in the throes of caring for a dying loved one.

ISBN 978-1-61722-149-1
148 pages • softcover • $19.95

Companioning the Grieving Child
A Soulful Guide for Caregivers

Renowned author and educator Dr. Alan Wolfelt redefines the role of the grief counselor in this guide for caregivers to grieving children. Providing a viable alternative to the limitations of the medical establishment's model for companioning the bereaved, Dr. Wolfelt encourages counselors and other caregivers to aspire to a more compassionate philosophy in which the child is the expert of his or her grief—not the counselor or caregiver. The approach outlined in the book argues against treating grief as an illness to be diagnosed and treated but rather for acknowledging it as an experience that forever changes a child's worldview. By promoting careful listening and observation, this guide shows caregivers, family members, teachers, and others how to support grieving children and help them grow into healthy adults.

ISBN 978-1-61722-158-3
160 pages • hardcover • $29.95

Companion
PRESS

All publications can be ordered by mail from:

Companion Press
3735 Broken Bow Road
Fort Collins, CO 80526
Phone: (970) 226-6050
Fax: 1-800-922-6051
www.centerforloss.com

The Companioning the Grieving Child Curriculum Book

Activities to Help Children and Teens Heal

BY PATRICIA MORRISSEY, M.S. ED.
FOREWORD BY ALAN D. WOLFELT, PH.D.

Based on Dr. Wolfelt's six needs of mourning and written to pair with *Companioning the Grieving Child*, this comprehensive guide provides hundreds of hands-on activities tailored for grieving children in three age groups: preschool, elementary, and teens. Through the use of readings, games, discussion questions, and arts and crafts, counselors will help grieving young people acknowledge the reality of the death, embrace the pain of the loss, remember the person who died, develop a new self-identity, search for meaning, and accept support from others.

Sample activities include:

- Grief sock puppets
- Tissue paper butterflies in conjunction with the picture book *My, Oh My—A Butterfly!*
- Expression bead bracelets
- The nurturing game
- Write an autobiopoem

Throughout the book, the theme of butterflies reminds readers that just as butterflies go through metamorphosis, so do grieving children. Activities are in an easy-to-follow format, each with a goal, objective, sequential description of the activity, and a list of needed materials.

ISBN 978-1-61722-185-9
208 pages • softcover • $29.95

Companion
PRESS

All publications can be ordered by mail from:

Companion Press
3735 Broken Bow Road
Fort Collins, CO 80526
Phone: (970) 226-6050
Fax: 1-800-922-6051
www.centerforloss.com

Companioning at a Time of Perinatal Loss

A Guide for Nurses, Physicians, Social Workers and Chaplains in the Hospital Setting

By Jane Heustis & Marcia Meyer Jenkins

Foreword by Alan D. Wolfelt, Ph.D.

The OB unit is the only hospital environment where life begins and, sometimes, tragically ends. Staff must alternate masks of comedy and tragedy as they care for the estimated 2-4 percent of deliveries that end in the death of a baby. Many OB caregivers feel unprepared to handle the intensity of perinatal loss. Most hospitals have bereavement care standards but offer little instruction in following them.

Written by seasoned support nurses, *Companioning at a Time of Perinatal Loss* outlines a framework for bereavement care in the obstetrical arena. Based on Dr. Alan Wolfelt's principles of companioning, it describes loss from the family's perspective, defines the caregiver's role, offers bedside strategies and reviews the work of mourning in the weeks and months after. Real-life stories teach what is important during times of intense sorrow.

ISBN 978-1-879651-47-0
144 pages • softcover • $19.95

All publications can be ordered by mail from:

Companion Press

3735 Broken Bow Road
Fort Collins, CO 80526

Phone: (970) 226-6050
Fax: 1-800-922-6051

www.centerforloss.com

Eight Critical Questions for Mourners…

And the Answers That Will Help You Heal

When loss enters your life, you are faced with many choices. The questions you ask and the choices you make will determine whether you become among the "living dead" or go on to live until you die. If you are going to integrate grief into your life, it helps to recognize what questions to ask yourself on the journey.

1. Will I grieve or mourn this loss?
2. Will I befriend my feelings of loss, or will I inhibit them?
3. Will I be a passive witness or an active participant in my grief?
4. Will I embrace the uniqueness of my grief?
5. Will I work on the six needs of mourning, or will I fall victim to the cliché "time heals all wounds?"
6. Will I believe I must achieve resolution, or will I work toward reconciliation?
7. Will I embrace my transformation?
8. Will this loss add to my "divine spark" or will it take away my life force?

This book provides the answers that will help you clarify your experiences and encourage you to make choices that honor the transformational nature of grief and loss.

ISBN 978-1-879651-62-3
176 pages • softcover • $18.95

Healing Your Traumatized Heart
100 Practical Ideas After Someone You Love Dies a Sudden, Violent Death

Death is never easy, but for families and friends affected by a sudden, violent death, grief is especially traumatic. Deaths caused by accidents, homicide, and suicide violate our moral, spiritual, and social codes. Things are not the same, nor will they ever be again. Persistent thoughts and feelings about what the death may have been like for the person who died—and what might have been done to prevent it—color the grief process. Strong feelings of anger and regret are also common. Understanding and expressing these feelings helps survivors, over time and with the support of others, come to reconcile their loss.

Most books about trauma are written for mental health caregivers. This book is for the mourner. It offers 100 practical ideas to help them through their traumatic loss. Some of the ideas explore the basic principles of traumatic grief and mourning. The remainder give practical, proactive suggestions for moving beyond the trauma and embracing their grief.

ISBN 978-1-879651-32-6
128 pages • softcover • $11.95

Companion
PRESS

All publications can be ordered by mail from:

Companion Press

3735 Broken Bow Road
Fort Collins, CO 80526

Phone: (970) 226-6050
Fax: 1-800-922-6051

www.centerforloss.com